BLIND AMBITION

Wendi Hayman

Publications

Printed in the United States of America
First Printing, 2017
ISBN 978-0-9982435-2-8
Published by:
Glory to Glory Publications, LLC
P.O. Box 855
Clayton, DE 19938
info@glorytoglorypublications.com
www.GlorytoGloryPublications.com
www.WendiHayman.com

Cover Design: Ed Wolfe at blazingcovers@gmail.com

This is a work of creative nonfiction. The events are of the author's life and experiences. While all the stories in this book are true, some names and identifying details used were to recreate events, locales, and conversations from memories of them and are in no way meant to defame any person, or place.

I dedicate this book to the loving memory of my father, Caleb Morrow, Jr. Daddy, you always believed in me, and you told me when I was just a teenager that I was supposed to be a writer. Although it took 30 plus years, I became just what you said I would be because it was ultimately God's purpose for my life.

Let's Stay Connected
Follow me on

Wendi Hayman
www.wendihayman.com

Acknowledgements

This book went through a long, tough labor, but I thank God for its birth. All the glory goes to my Lord and Savior, Jesus Christ. I thank God for giving me the strength and courage to be transparent to write and share my story. It surely wasn't easy, I learned a lot about myself during this writing, and was healed and delivered in areas that I discovered were deep rooted.

This book is dedicated to my husband, Tom Hayman, my girls, Marcia and Donye', my mother, Ora Morrow, my family, friends, and church family for believing in me and supporting me throughout this process. I thank Tom for trusting the vision that God has given me for ministry and business and for being supportive as I venture into all that God has called me to do. Also, for your support in the long nights of writing, typing, and reading, as well as travel, and the many courses and calls with my writing/publishing mentor, Tressa Smallwood, whom I am also grateful for. Thank you, Tom, for your encouragement for the many times I wanted to quit. I thank you Donye' for encouraging me and always cheering me on. Thank you, Marcia, for being patient, understanding, and dedicated to this process with me. I also thank you for the time you took off your daughter and editor hat, and put on the hat as a true woman of God and ministered to me and spoke into my life to push through the pain and get the book out.

I want to honor Bishop I.V. and Pastor Bridget Hilliard; for it is their ministry and teaching that gave me the spiritual foundation that set the course for my journey restored by grace, and to live a life of faith.

I want to thank Terri Townsend and Tamika Collick for being the advanced readers and editors of this book. I thank my prayer partner, Lorena Wooten, and Jamie Holmes for being a friend, support, encourager, confidant, and cheerleader. A special thank you to my sister, Ethel Hunter, for being my midwife to the birthing of this book, my mentors, Pastor Beverly Mahoney and Dr. A. Renee Cooper, and my spiritual mother, Minister Pamela Price for always being there when I needed you, a listening ear, a voice of reason, and always imparting the word of God in me when I needed it the most.

To anyone who I did not specifically name, but you have supported me, encouraged me, and prayed for me, I would like to thank you and know that you are loved.

Dear Reader,

Society tells us that we should follow our heart, do what makes us happy, or do what we're passionate about, but doing so may not necessarily be the purpose for your life. Then, there are many of us who don't do any of these; we just get a job and go through life working a nine to five until it's time to retire. We get content, sometimes even complacent, and we do not discover that we have a deeper purpose than just working a job to get a paycheck to pay our bills so that our everyday living expenses and necessities are sustained. We were designed to be greater, to do more, and to make an impact.

Have you ever pursued something that you felt so strongly about? Did you put a lot of time, effort, energy, and even money into it only to have things not work out the way you initially expected? Taking a journey that is guided by your self-interests may lead you on a path that you were never intended to be on. It may end up costing you mentally, emotionally, but more importantly, spiritually. Life is full of choices, and the decisions we make can either give us life or bring death both spiritually and naturally.

Consequently, we feel that we are capable of making our own choices, especially regarding what we want to do with our lives. This is quite the contrary. God created us and established His purpose in us before the foundation of the earth. Therefore, He wants our lives to be led by Him. Our lives are designed by God so that He gets the glory out of everything that we do. Not often when we go through life do we actually take the time to ask God what His purpose is for us. We don't stop to find out if He has a purpose for that career, business, or relationship that we were pursuing.

Growing up, I had a passion for dance and ambition to reach my heart's desire of being a famous dancer, but at the same time, I was too blind to see that the path I had taken was not what I envisioned for myself. The ambition I chose to follow took me on a journey far from God's purpose for my life.

Blind Ambition is the essence of my story; my journey from and back to my purpose. It tells how I allowed blind ambition to lead me to pursue something that I had a strong desire for, only to find myself in places that I was not meant to be. During the pursuit of this ambition, I went on a journey that led me further away from God and His purpose for my life. But God, who is rich in grace and mercy, divinely orchestrated things in my life to set me on a path that would cause me to run into His love for me, which got me back on track to my pathway to purpose. This book is to guide and aid you to deeply seek God and ask Him to reveal His ordained purpose for your life.

☙ Intro ❧

I'd heard that rap artists, music producers, record company execs, or industry personnel frequented strip clubs all the time. As I mounted the stage at *Fantasy,* my first night there, I did so with a goal and one goal only: to be discovered. The beat dropped, and Ginuwine's *Pony* blared through the club's speakers. I nervously danced around the pole and onto other areas of the stage. I continued to dance seductively as "If you're horny let's do it" rang out before I dropped down into a squat position gyrating my hips as "ride it, my pony" followed. I danced the best I could through my nervousness. As the music continued, dancing around the stage, I tugged at the strings tied around my neck, and my top fell suddenly. I just let it hang in that position because I was too nervous, shamed, and embarrassed to take it off any further. As the song neared its end, and men stood at the bottom of the stage, money in hand, I knew they wanted more. I had to give more. *Fantasy* was after all an all-nude strip club. I had to give them the fantasy they came for and would ultimately pay for.

My focus was not on the men or their money. I loved to dance, and I was a darn good dancer. The music videos and award shows I watched growing up had me wanting nothing more than to be dancing background for a rapper. But how did I end up here, on a stage, dancing in the nude? I was a hip-hop dancer and that was what I was really working towards. I knew all the latest hip-hop songs and all the latest and greatest hip-hop dance moves. Nonetheless, there I stood on stage in 6" heels, minus the pink mesh G-string and bikini top I had on when I first got there, twirling around a pole while men threw money at me. I watched it all fall onto the stage as I continued to dance.

ᕦ The Decoy Seed ᕤ

Paul knew that in the position that he was in, there was an
opportunity that he could exalt himself. Paul was inflicted by a
messenger of Satan and sought the Lord to deliver him from the
affliction. God allowed this affliction upon Paul to show forth the
***purpose** of His grace, which is sufficient for us regardless of what*
situations or circumstances we find ourselves in, in life.
(2 Corinthians 12:7)

We are often shaped by our environments, the people
closest to us, those we admire, and what we see and
experience. Seeds are sown into us and watered by life
experiences, by what we see and hear. When seeds are
watered, they become thoughts, and those thoughts
permeate through our soul, and eventually develop our
character, personality, and actions. I grew up in the church,
and I knew what it meant to live a holy and godly lifestyle;
however, seeds of iniquity, familial spirits, and other life
experiences prohibited me from fully living according to the
principles I had been taught.

At a very young age, while I was still in elementary
school, I was exposed to pornography when I stumbled
upon some pornographic magazines hidden in our home. As
a young child, I engaged in activities that children called
"playing house" with the action of "humping" with friends
in the neighborhood. *How do kids learn to do such things at*

young ages? I was also exposed to drugs and alcohol from weekend visits with my dad.

Growing up, I spent the majority of my summers in Louisiana with my mom's side of the family. I really enjoyed my visits to Louisiana, and I looked forward to going every summer, which I did until I was 16 years old. During those times I was away from home in Louisiana, I was exposed to negative behaviors such as teenage sex, drugs, alcohol, and inappropriate touching from older female family members whom I looked up to.

I had a favorite cousin who I spent most my time with. Many of the behaviors I acted out in my life were because of influences from my cousin. She and I got along really well and liked a lot of the same things. I endeavored to be like her in every way. I wanted to act, talk, and dress like her, and I especially wanted to associate with boys like her. Her character, actions, and the choices she made didn't make her a good example, but I wanted to be like her anyway. Since I looked up to her so much, I didn't question the inappropriate acts she pulled me into: hanging out with boys, underage drinking, and sexual acts with her and boys. In high school, my cousin was a band member and a dancer at her high school in Louisiana; I was in band at my high school in Houston. She became pregnant as a teenager; after my first semester of high school, I also became pregnant. Without question, my wanting to be like my cousin encouraged many of my actions as a teenager. These actions transitioned into my young adult and eventually adulthood life.

Even though I frequently witnessed drug and alcohol use as a child, it did not have a major effect on my life. At age 12, my dad had a talk with me and told me never to drink, smoke, or do drugs of which I obeyed. Years later, he also told me not to have sex; however, the seed of the perverse spirit had already taken root in me during my childhood.

Growing up, I also dealt with abandonment and rejection issues. I did not have a good relationship with my mother. I did not feel like I had a mother's love because she was very angry due to two failed marriages, and I was the recipient of her anger through excessive beatings. I had four older siblings who did not live in the home with my mother and me. When my sisters would visit on the weekend, there was often sibling rivalry between myself and my sister closest to me in age.

Although he was not in the home, my father and I had a very close and loving relationship. However, there were times when I felt abandoned and rejected by him after he married another woman and had a family with her and her kids; I went through this cycle twice. My father also disappeared from my life for a three-year period and didn't return until my senior year of high school. I also suffered from rejection from my father's side of the family as well. On my dad's side of the family, I have a cousin who was born four days before me; however, I was not treated with the same love as my cousin from my grandmother and aunts. Only one of my dad's sisters treated my cousin and me with equal love.

The adult behaviors and activities I witnessed and was exposed to as a kid and young teen opened the door to unhealthy behaviors in my life: lust, perversion, promiscuity, and pornography. I also developed low self-esteem, and that, along with feelings of abandonment and rejection, propelled the sexual perversion of promiscuity with males that would follow me throughout the years of my life.

Purpose Principle

The behaviors I witnessed coupled with the issues that I faced early in life became the decoy to my life going in the wrong direction. Although I excelled in school, was a good person, and succeeded in several areas of my life, the seeds of iniquity that were sown into me at an early age laid dormant until further life's experiences watered them until the time of increase, which yielded the fruits of the spirit of perversion.

The seeds that are sown into us, decoys that come into our lives, especially early in life, are designed to derail us from our purpose that was preordained by God. Seeds, both positive and negative, are sown into us all the time from people, our home life, and society. The seeds that are sown into our lives early can determine the path our life will take, and the seed that is cultivated the most, either negative or positive, will have the dominant effect. We have to be careful of which of these seeds are allowed to take root and thrive in us. Any negative seed we allow to take root and is cultivated by our life's experiences will always produce an unexpected and unwanted harvest. Only the positive seeds that we allow to take root and are positively cultivated will produce a purposeful harvest. The fruit of our life should be one that is yielded by purpose.

Our life's experiences, how we act and think, and what we become are from the culmination of seeds sown into us. The seed of our purpose was planted in us before we were even born, as shown in the example of the prophet Jeremiah's life (Jeremiah 1:5). However, the enemy to our purpose comes immediately to manifest deception or to derail our purpose just as it did with Jeremiah when he said that he could not speak because he was a child (Jeremiah 1:6). The decoy to purpose comes in various forms very early on in our lives. It can manifest through sexual perversions to a child, rejection, abandonment, or trauma. Later in life, some experience traumatic events such as rape, sudden death, or abuse, as well as disappointments and bad choices that can also become decoys to purpose.

The decoys that enter our lives are designed to derail us from God's original intent for our life, and therefore, force us to go through life trying to make our own way or create our own purpose. We then establish a purpose for our life based on personal beliefs, feelings, emotions, and experiences and not on what God has ordained us to do.

❧ The Root of Rejection ☙

*Jesus was our ultimate example of being rejected. He went through shame, pain, and suffering. This was for the **purpose** of redeeming mankind back to God. (Isaiah 53:3-12)*

The very first time I had sex, I ended up pregnant because I was in the wrong place doing the wrong thing. I was spending some time at one of my sister's apartment, and while at the pool one day, I met this guy, who I had some fun playing around with in the pool. That evening, my sister was going to church and asked if I wanted to go. I said no and told her I would stay home. After she left, I called the guy who I met at the pool, and he came over. While he was there, we had unprotected sex. The next day, I went over to his apartment, and we had sex again, but this time he had a condom. Yeah, we did it backwards because by then it was a little too late.

When I had an inclination that I was pregnant due to a missed menstrual cycle, I did not know how to handle it or how to tell my mother. At first, I was in denial that I could be pregnant, so I made up all kinds of scenarios in my mind that could explain my situation. I was just gaining weight because I was eating too many snacks. But as the months went by, and I still didn't have a cycle, I couldn't deny it anymore. So, I came up with a plan for my mother to find out. I ran track in middle school, and I had planned to do so

10

in high school as well. My plan was to wait until I went to get my physical for track. I knew that when the doctor did my exam, he would make a note that I was pregnant, and that would be how my mother would find out and that's exactly how she did.

When I came out of the doctor's office, my mother asked for my physical paper. I told her the doctor kept the form because I might be about 5 months pregnant. My mother was furious. She asked why I didn't tell her that I was pregnant so that I could have gotten an abortion. That is exactly why I didn't tell her. My mother and I never ever talked about sex or anything, but I feared that if she found out, abortion might have been her solution. So, I didn't tell her on purpose for fear of not wanting to have an abortion. She was so mad that she wouldn't even take me home. She pulled the car over to a pay phone to call my daddy at work and let him know that she was bringing me to him. My daddy was just as furious that his baby girl, and only child, could have done something like this. Especially since he had told me before that boys only wanted to use girls to relieve themselves, and I should not let them use me. I didn't listen. I had gotten caught up with all the sexual activity that I witnessed going on around me, and I succumbed to the unspoken peer pressure.

My daddy was married to his third wife at the time. She had four children, two of which lived with them. My weekend visits weren't all that amazing, but I enjoyed my time with my daddy. Sometimes I got to do fun things while hanging out with my step-sister and cousins from their side of the family. For the most part, I wasn't treated badly, but I felt like I was treated like the stepchild versus being the biological child.

My mama didn't want to face the shame and embarrassment of her teenaged daughter being pregnant, so I could no longer stay at her house. During the Christmas break, I packed my clothes, and she shipped me to my daddy's house. However, I was only there during a waiting period until a bed became available at the adoption agency home that I would be living at. Not only were they not going to let me live with them, but they were also making me give my baby up for adoption.

What made matters worse was that my step sister was pregnant also. She and I went to the same school for pregnant teens. However, she was allowed to stay home at my daddy's house and keep her baby. This really broke me as a young girl and made me have ill feelings towards my daddy. Especially because he and I had a great relationship; my relationship with my daddy was better than the one I had with my mother. Imagine how this could make a young, teenage girl feel. Not only did my parents not want me, but they were also making me give away my baby. I was sad, alone, hurt, broken, abandoned, and rejected at a time when I needed my parents the most.

When I moved into the adoption agency home, I had to make a life for myself all on my own. I had no option but to become friends and family with about 25 other pregnant teenagers who were planning to give their babies up for adoption. There were also girls there who went to school with us but were keeping their babies. This was a very difficult and emotional period of my life. My mother and father kept my pregnancy a secret from everyone, so I didn't have much support from other family members. The girls and I had to lean on one another, and we became a support system to each other since this was a very difficult period to go through alone. The home wasn't too bad though. The staff took us on various outings to the movies, to the mall, and out to eat to give us some social activities, but we had to earn these outings by keeping our grades up, doing our chores, and getting along with others.

We would hear of girls who delivered their babies, and once they laid eyes on them, they had a change of heart and didn't give their baby up for adoption as they planned to do.

My roommate and I had become close friends, and we felt like sisters. We fought and got into disagreements, but we would always make up. We even continued our friendship long after we left the home. She had her baby first and stuck to the plan of adoption. It was difficult for her, but I was there for her. When it was my turn, I wasn't at all prepared for the adoption of my daughter.

I attended my weekly counseling sessions with my adoption agent who worked at getting me prepared for the process. Even my parents and baby's father were counseled on the adoption process. However, up until I gave birth, I hadn't signed any adoption papers. Before I gave birth, my daughter's father decided he wanted her. My mother agreed with this idea, but I wasn't too sure I wanted her to live with them. I didn't like their living conditions. My father wanted to still go through with the adoption process. I was torn in different directions. A few weeks prior to my daughter's birth, my aunt, my father's sister, had called to talk to me. She said that she wouldn't mind taking the baby in and raising her. I told her that I would talk to my parents and get back to her.

My due date had passed, and she still hadn't shown up. She must have known that there were no solid plans for where she would live upon her arrival. After being two weeks past due, I was scheduled for an induced labor. My mama picked me up from the home and took me to the hospital. We arrived around 6pm that evening. I got checked into a room, examined, and then my water was broken. When they broke my water, nothing came out. They found that I had no more fluid which was why I hadn't gone into labor on my own. The nurses told my mama that it would be hours before I would go into labor, so she left me there by myself and went to run errands. The nurses asked if I wanted an epidural, and I declined because I wasn't feeling any pain. Besides, I was scared to get it because I heard horror stories from people who had gotten it. Every time the nurses checked on me, they would show me on the monitor that I was having contractions, but I never felt anything.

About two hours after I was induced, a nurse came to check me, and I was dilated 9cm. She told me, "You are almost ready to deliver this baby, and you haven't felt any contractions?" I told her no, but I asked if I could still have that epidural. She told me no because it was too late and the baby was on the way. They then prepped me to start pushing before the doctor came in to deliver the baby. As I laid there, a 15-year-old teenager all alone getting ready to deliver my baby, I was overcome with emotion. I recalled my Lamaze breathing exercises every time I was told to push. I pushed and grunted when I was instructed. The nurses told me I could scream and holler, but I was afraid to because I didn't want to be embarrassed. My daughter's head was a little bit larger than I could push out, so I had to have a 4-degree episiotomy. After I had delivered a 6lb 9oz healthy baby girl, the nurses turned to me and said, "You were the best patient we have ever had." I responded, "You mean the best teenage patient." They said, "No, the best patient ever." That was surprising, especially since I didn't know what I was doing. After the delivery, I called my mother, who was at home, and told her that I had my baby. She was upset because she expected it to be hours. I called my baby's father and my daddy as well.

When it was time for us to be discharged from the hospital, it was chaotic in my room. My mother, my father, the adoption agent, and one of my aunts were all in my room. Then, my baby's father and his grandfather showed up in anticipation of taking our daughter home. When I saw he had a sheet and a pillowcase in lieu of a car seat, I knew I could not let her leave with him. The adoption agent was pressing for a signature on the adoption papers as previously agreed. There were so many different conversations going on around me, and everyone was pressing me for a decision. I was a confused ball of emotions.

While everyone was talking, I reached over and grabbed the hospital phone, called my other aunt whom I previously spoken to, and asked her if she wanted my baby. She excitedly responded yes. I hung up the phone and told everyone that my baby and I will be going to my aunt's house, and she will take her. This didn't sit too well with my parents, and especially not well with the adoption agent, who was really upset. However, I got out of bed, gathered my belongings and my baby, and left the hospital. My daughter and I went to stay with my aunt. I stayed with my aunt for several months to assist with my newborn baby. After I left the house and moved back to my mother's, I would visit regularly, pick my daughter up for weekend visits with me, and when my daddy would pick me up for his weekend visits, my daughter would come right along with me. I remained a constant in her life. I even later found out that my mother would sneak over to my aunt's house for visits.

Still, no one in my family knew I had had a baby. When she would come over, we would just tell everyone that she was my aunt's daughter, and no one asked any further questions. Except for my grandmother. I recall one visit to Louisiana during my pregnancy. We were preparing to leave, and I was in the kitchen ironing my clothes when my grandmother came over to me and said, "You take care of that baby now." I said nothing because I didn't think she knew. She knew, but no one had told her. I asked my mama if she told my grandmother about my pregnancy, and she said no; it was just that old wise woman intuition.

It wasn't until my daughter was about 12 years old that we revealed her to my siblings and their families. She and I had been separated for a few years following a fight I had with my aunt. After I gave my life to Christ, was growing in the word of God, and developing my faith, I used my faith to find my daughter's whereabouts. After we were reunited, we have had a relationship ever since.

This experience was a true source of rejection in my life that ran deep. I never talked about it or told anyone about this period in my life, but it has had a major effect on me. It made me feel unloved and unwanted because of a mistake I made. From that point on, I had to do everything just right. My grades had to be high, and I had to keep my associations with boys limited, or at least publicly, because after I'd gotten that first taste of sex, it didn't stop there. My mother put me on birth control pills, so I didn't have to be concerned about getting pregnant again. But my experiences with rejection didn't end after the birth of my daughter.

I started a new high school my sophomore year and was in band. There was this bass drummer who had caught my eye. To me, he was good looking, and he was fierce on that bass drum. He and I became friends in band because he seemed to always have a girlfriend. I didn't really have a boyfriend, but I was talking to someone. He and I had become really close friends. When he and one of his girlfriend broke up, I made it known that I wanted to be his girlfriend, but he wouldn't let me. I couldn't understand that. I wanted to be a part of his life so badly, so I made a vow that if I couldn't be his girlfriend then I would be his best friend, and so best friends we became. However, our relationship was like we were boyfriend and girlfriend, even though he did have a girlfriend. We did just about everything together.

However, I never felt like I could be myself around him. I never wanted to upset him or do anything that would cause him to eject me from his life. If he did or said something to make me upset or that I didn't like, I wouldn't speak up or say anything. I never let my true feelings be known to him even though we were good friends.

When he graduated the year before me, I went my separate way, met a guy, and was in a relationship to the point we had gotten engaged after I graduated high school. I went away to college and had gotten caught up in the college life, and that four-year relationship ended. After that, I had met the guy who I would have a baby with and eventually marry. When things went south in our marriage, I ran to my best friend, and he was there for me. During my time of distress, he and I did something we had never done before in all our years of friendship; we had sex. It was an experience for the both of us. I confessed my actions to my husband, and he decided that he did not want to get back together. So, I basically became the "other woman" once again in my best friend's life because he had a girlfriend. When we got back together this time, we were going strong now with sex added to the mix. We did everything together, and I even went on his drug runs with him. I was also a staple in his family. I was at every birthday party and holiday dinner, and I regularly visited his family's home. His girlfriend didn't like it, but she learned that Wendi was a fixture in his life and wasn't going away.

We got separated again when he went to jail for drugs. He contacted me and told me he had gotten locked up, which was after I hadn't heard from him after some time had passed. During that year, I had given my life to Christ. Since I was on his visitors list, a couple of Sundays out the month, I would make the four-hour drive with my daughter to visit him. I would send him letters and cards regularly to let him know that I was thinking of him, to encourage him, and let him know that I would be there for him when he got released. Once during a visit, I ministered to him, and he gave his heart to Christ by saying the prayer of salvation. When he got released, he immediately came to visit me. I was ecstatic. Even though I was newly saved and had made the vow to not have sex, I had sex with him that night. But then, the devastation and rejection came. He still had both me and the other girl. Due to my visits to the prison and constant communication, his feelings for me had grown to another level and mine had also. I told him he had to make a decision on which one of us he was going to continue a relationship with. He decided it was her. This devastated me. This was when I went away for good, and she no longer had to worry about me. I couldn't even remain friends with him knowing that I had put my heart and soul into him and was still rejected.

There was rejection deeply rooted in my relationship with him, and I took it into other relationships and interactions with guys. I didn't want to be rejected. I didn't want to know that a guy possibly wouldn't want me, so I would do just about anything to not be rejected; especially having sex with a guy for the first time meeting them. If I really liked a guy and was really into him, I would restrain myself from expressing any dislikes or disagreements to avoid rejection. Eventually, I got bold, and I started being the one to reject men. I would have sex with a guy and not call him again. I would have a mean, nasty attitude and not

19

care about their feelings. I flipped the script on rejection, and I put up a brick and steel wall around my heart and adopted a hard exterior. I would get questioned so much about why I didn't smile. People, especially strangers, would always say to me, "Why do you look so mean? You need to smile. You are too pretty not to smile." Well, I didn't believe that anyway because of my low self-esteem. I would not let anyone penetrate through my heart because I refused to be rejected again. Even when I did get into long-term, steady relationships, I maintained my hard exterior and kept the wall around my heart. I had to protect myself. I stayed this way for many years. I rejected numerous people and relationships, and I ran off good people from my life in an erroneous effort to reject rejection. During a self-evaluation study one year when I was taking anger management classes, God showed me that I had a fear of rejection and that was why I responded to and treated people the way I did. So, I prayed and asked God to free me from rejection. I wanted to be a better person not only for myself but as a representative of Christ.

Purpose Principle

The rejection that happens in our lives has the potential to affect our purpose in several ways. Rejection can rob us of our purpose, paralyze us from moving forward in it, or cause us to simply not follow purpose at all. Rejection can bring with it a level of fear, including the fear of rejection, fear of the unknown, and fear of failure.

Know that rejection is an enemy to purpose. If you have experienced rejection in any area of your life, and it has taken root and affects how you live, behave, and interact with others, you cannot remain the same. You must uproot rejection from your heart and life. Sometimes rejection can lie dormant, and we do not realize it until we want to do something different, start something new such as a business or go to school, or even get into a different type of relationship.

Joseph was rejected by his brothers after he revealed to them the dream God had given him, which basically translated that he would rule over them. He was also thrown in jail after being falsely accused and then forgotten about in jail. This could have really affected and altered God's purpose for his life. However, Joseph kept his focus on his purpose, and he did not allow what he went through to deter him. Ultimately, he reached his purposed destiny and fulfilled God's plan for his life.

No matter what has gone on in our lives, we must know and understand that God's purpose for us must prevail. We cannot allow anything that has happened to us, how others have treated us, or anyone who opposes our purpose to get us off focus. We must remain firmly fixed on the purpose and promise of God, and we must do all that we can to fulfill it.

Rejection has to be ejected from our souls. We must know who we are and that we are here for a purpose to fulfill a specific and unique plan for our lives. We can't keep ourselves back from living out our God given purpose based on our past mistakes or experiences. We must release the issues of the past, especially rejection and people who have rejected us, and forgive so that we can move forward in life with purposeful intent to live out purpose to our full potential.

Ꮹ The Decoy Discovery Ꮱ

*Moses was discovered by Pharaoh's daughter who raised him as her son (Exodus 2:6-10). This discovery was orchestrated by God because of His **purpose** for Moses' life. Moses had killed an Egyptian and fled from Pharaoh's house, but God **purposed** for Moses to be the one to deliver His people, the children of Israel, out of Egypt from the bondage of Pharaoh. (Exodus 3:10-12).*

When I was around nine years old, I discovered I had a natural talent for dancing. Whenever I heard music, I would just dance. At first, I played my mom's old albums and made up dance steps to the music. Years later, I received a radio as a Christmas gift, and from then on, all I would do is listen to the radio and make up dance routines. I loved to dance and became very passionate about it. One thing that my cousin in Louisiana and I had in common was that she also liked to dance. She and I would go to parties, the skating rink, and although we weren't old enough, the clubs. We did a lot of dancing together in our teenage years, and we reaped a lot of attention. Unbeknownst to me, a seed had been planted, and I developed a mindset and need for attention.

When I was in elementary school, my parents sent me to a magnet (specialty) school outside of my local neighborhood where I enrolled in band. I really didn't want to be in band, so I selected what I thought would be an easy instrument to play, the flute, which turned out not to be so easy after all. Moving on to middle school, I had to pick two electives, so I selected dance as my first choice. Unfortunately for me, I had to audition and did not get selected because I had no prior dance training. I was forced back into band, and this time, I had to put more effort into learning the music. When it was time for me to move into high school, I begged my parents to allow me to go to a school that had a cosmetology program. I enjoyed doing hair, which was also something that my favorite cousin did. As I said, I wanted to be just like her. My parents said no and told me that I had to attend a school that had an honors program or that offered advanced college preparatory classes. This worked out well since I went on to graduate in the top 10% and #15 of my class.

So, I found a high school in my local neighborhood that was also well known for their band. I was excited to join band in high school because I had been to football games, and I saw how during halftime show the band would play popular songs, perform dances, and get the crowd hyped. Unfortunately, things didn't go as I expected. During my freshman year, our school got a new band director, and he was firmly against the halftime dance. As a matter-of-fact, he did not even allow us to play popular songs in which bands were known to play at football games. My freshman year of high school band was disastrous and not as exciting as I thought it would be. However, because I became pregnant after my first semester, I couldn't remain at public high school anyway.

Sophomore year after I had my baby, I transferred to a school closer to home, and I started playing with the band in the summer. I was now excited to be in high school band. The drum majors were very talented, and the band dances were the best. I really wanted to be a part of the band, but I didn't want to play an instrument. The dance team wasn't any good, so I didn't want to join them. So, I auditioned to be a twirler mainly because I liked the skimpy outfits; however, I didn't make the team, so I was stuck playing an instrument. During practice, I initially had a hard time learning the music, but that didn't bother me because I quickly learned the choreography of the band dance.

Dancing was my passion, and I gave it my all at every practice, football game, parade, band competition, and school dance. I proved my dance skills and swiftly garnered the attention of male band members and eventually others, although I received negative attention from many girls in school. I enjoyed the attention and praise that I received when I danced, especially from the boys. This caused me to become promiscuous with several guys in band and in school until I got into a serious relationship in my junior year that lasted four years.

I made sure to give maximum effort with every opportunity I was given to dance. The band became my life, and the attention became my fuel, so I worked hard to excel in band, especially the dance portion of performances. I had evolved into a pretty good flute player as well, remaining between first, second, or third chair during my band tenure.

I remained in band only throughout my junior year. Even though I was no longer in band, I still hung out with my band mates, attended band activities and events, and continued traveling with them to parades and competitions. Second semester of my junior year, I enrolled into my high school's Office Education program in which I was fortunate enough to secure my very first job at the NASA Johnson Space Center. I started work at NASA during the summer prior to my senior year and throughout.

When our class took our senior trip to Orlando, FL for a week, our last stop was to Daytona Beach. While on the beach, some friends and I were approached to enter a dance contest called the "Swatch Watch Dance Contest." We decided to enter and join the fun, and we had an exciting time dancing against one another and strangers. There were multiple rounds where someone would get eliminated each round, and I made it through each round until I was 1 of the 2 people in the final round. I won 1st place in the dance contest, and I won a Swatch watch as the prize. That's how good I was at dancing, and I was just a high school student competing against college-age and older adults.

After I graduated high school and at the end of my term at NASA, I was offered a full-time position with the opportunity to go to college locally, but I declined and chose to go away to college instead. This was the first regretful mistake I made in life, which I strongly believe would have saved me from the journey that I later embarked upon.

In preparing for college, I was eager to become a part of a college band because of some performances I had witnessed at college football games I attended. College bands were on another level and performed on a grander scale than high school, so going to college was going to be great, or so I thought. Unfortunately, I allowed my parents to influence my college career path, and I chose pharmacy as a major. I decided to go to Xavier University of New Orleans because they had a top pharmacy program, but the school did not have a band.

What the school did have was parties and lots of them. I learned this during freshman orientation. Matter-of-fact, at the end of the freshmen orientation, the DJ put on music and the MC urged us to come out to the gym floor and dance. At first, I was not going to go out and dance because I was in a new environment, but at the urging of my mother, I made my way to the dance floor and quickly made my mark in the freshman class at Xavier. I became known as the freshman girl from Houston who could dance, and thus, I quickly had college party buddies. Even better, New Orleans was party central with all the college parties, all-nighter parties, Mardi Gras parades and parties, house parties, and the famous French Quarter. I took part in all of them. I spent my first semester of college attending more parties then I did studying.

Many college students party to drink, but I partied to dance; I did not drink because dancing was my drink and my drug. While attending these parties, I discovered a popular local dance referred to as the *p-pop*, a dance similar to twerking. When I first saw this dance, I was determined to learn it. Practicing in my dorm room every opportunity I got, I not only learned the dance, I perfected it. I had perfected the dance so well that whenever I did the *p-pop* at parties, people thought I was a native of New Orleans.

My first semester grades reflected exactly how much I partied and didn't study, so my mom threatened to make me come back home if I didn't improve my grades the next semester. I quickly found a balance between studying and partying because there was no way that I was going to give up the freedom I had gained while being away in college. In high school, the band was an outlet for me because my mom was mean, strict, and would not always allow me to go to the school dances or parties. Most of my high school social life was stifled by always having to babysit my younger sister. So, I was definitely not willing to risk my freedom to go back home.

CR My Self-Proclaimed Purpose ℘

*God even had a **purpose** for a harlot. Rahab was used to hide
the spies sent out by Joshua to view the land in which God
promised the children of Israel, and she received the favor of the
Lord for her and her household. (Joshua 2:1, 12-14)*

We didn't have cable television growing up; in fact,
my mother still doesn't have it to this day. Visits to relatives'
homes gave me glimpses of what cable television had to
offer. I remember when I was around 15 and I saw my first
rap videos and a BET award show. I was so excited to see
the background dancers and seeing these videos and
performances led me to make a self-proclaimed purpose. I
declared that I wanted to be a background dancer. I thought
that if I became a background dancer and danced at
concerts, in rap videos, and on award shows, then maybe I
would have the attention from people that I longed for. I
would no longer feel lonely, rejected, or abandoned. The
reason I felt lonely and rejected is because growing up and
in school, I had very few female friends. I wasn't readily
accepted by girls, and if they did accept me, the friendships
never lasted. So, this led me to develop more relationships
with guys.

During my second semester in college, I had the
opportunity to attend a Greek step show and party on
Louisiana State University's campus. As soon as the party
started, I found my favorite place on the dance floor. If I

didn't have anyone to dance with, I would always just go out to the dance floor and start dancing alone. Then it would happen: the attention would be drawn to me and a circle would begin to form around me as I was dancing. This generally happened to me every time I danced at parties and clubs. After the circle formed, different guys would come in to dance with me or dance against me in a challenge, but I was always able to hold my own. My dancing at this particular party gained me the attention of a local rapper who was in attendance. During a conversation with him, he told me that he was looking for backup dancers; this was music to my ears. He and I exchanged information, and he also asked if I'd be able to recruit other girls from campus who would also be interested in auditioning. I was elated to finally get my chance to dance for a rapper.

Several weeks later, I went to audition for the rapper *Quiet Storm* and his manager, and I was selected on the spot. I was immediately thrust into the rap industry because *Quiet Storm* was an up-and-coming New Orleans rapper. We began attending studio recordings, practice sessions, concerts, and attending hip hop industry conferences together.

Eventually, he and I became a couple, which aligned with another desire of mine to marry a rap artist. My freshman year of college ended, but I remained in New Orleans for the summer to retake a failed class and to work on campus. I continued my relationship with *Quiet Storm* as his girlfriend and dancer. However, due to an issue with my roommate in our off-campus apartment and my inability to afford rent on my own, my mom decided it was best that I return to Houston. This was devastating to me, or so I thought. Returning to Houston was actually a setup on another road that would lead me closer to my *self-proclaimed* purpose.

Purpose Principle

We have to be careful and cognizant of what we speak. When you put out in the atmosphere the purpose that you proclaim for your life or your wants and desires, spiritual forces, whether angelic or demonic, go to work to guide you towards reaching that purpose. "A man's stomach shall be satisfied from the fruit of his mouth; from the produce of his life he shall be filled. Death and life are in the power of the tongue, and those who love it will eat its fruit." (Proverbs 18:20-21). When I proclaimed that I wanted to be a background dancer, the path had been set for me to get there, but it was the choices I made along the way that determined how I reached that destination or if I made the choices that would turn me back towards the path originally set for my life.

Oftentimes, we get off track from what we should be doing for what we want to do. God's plan for our life must take precedent over our own agenda. People have allowed society to deceive them into believing that they should put themselves first. God is first, and He must be allowed to have first place in your life. Doing anything outside of the plan and purpose of God will not bring fulfillment. Society has taught us that the way to fulfillment is following "your" dream, have a bank account full of money, live in a nice house, drive a nice car, wear designer clothes and shoes, travel, and make a name for yourself. This ideology has resulted in an abundance of reality TV shows that deceive people on what achieving success looks like.

These accomplishments and acquisitions don't bring total fulfillment because if they did, there would be a rest and a total peace to life. This is apparently not entirely accurate due to the amount of people in society who have riches but are alcoholics, drug addicts, or have committed suicide. If people would just search deep within themselves, they will find a longing for something more. It's unfortunate that we mistake that longing for more as the fulfillment of our desires, but that longing is God. He is tugging at your heart asking you to give him first place in your life.

A misconception that some people have is that if they put God first then they will miss out on something. Most of the time, these are longings of the flesh. The truth is that what you are doing is missing out on God and everything that He has for you. In God, all things and desires are fulfilled. "Delight yourself also in the Lord, and He shall give you the desires of your heart." (Psalms 37:5). Fleshly desires cannot replace the fulfillment of God.

At one point, I completely ignored the tugging by the spirit of God, and I was only causing more damage to myself. The longer you stay away from God, the further you stray, and the further away you are from God, you will continue to wander further down a path that was not intended for you. At some point, you will look at your current life and wonder, "How did I get here?"

☙ The Purpose Distraction ❧

*God decreed for the prophet Hosea to marry a woman, Gomer, who was a whore who kept leaving her husband to be with her lovers. God decreed for Hosea to love Gomer and get her back from her lover. This relationship was used by God for the **purpose** of showing the depth of the love that He had for the children of Israel although they had turned away from Him to worship Baal. (Hosea 1:2, 3:1-5; 14:1-2)*

After getting a taste of the rap industry, I wanted to be a part of that industry now more than ever. Back in Houston, I began to contact old acquaintances, and I connected with one who was the Director of a High School Leadership program that I was a part of during my senior year. During a conversation, he told me about how he'd started a record label and was working with a local rap group on their upcoming album. He mentioned that the group would soon be holding auditions for female backup dancers. Of course, this piqued my interest. I immediately expressed interest and requested the information, but he refused to give it to me. He explained that this group was not one that someone of my character should be associated with. However, I would not be denied, and I persisted. I knew that I had the dance skills, but he steadily refused my requests. Days later, I showed up at his office inquiring about the audition and begged until he reluctantly agreed. He gave me a flyer with the details of where the audition would be held. The auditions were for a group, the *Sexxx Fiends*, whose new single was very hot on the local radio station at the time. I hadn't heard of the group or their song yet, but I was still eager for this new dance opportunity not knowing the theme of the group or their music.

I went to the audition dressed in my hip hop style clothing, which was the way I dressed at the time; another emulation of my cousin. I performed a hip-hop dance, and the group and others judges were impressed. Several days later, I received a call saying they selected me for a second group audition with other girls whom they'd chosen. This second audition had different criteria than the first. At this audition, they wanted the dancers to wear sexy lingerie with a G-string. I didn't even really know what a G-string was let alone owned one. I immediately argued that I was a hip-hop dancer and couldn't dance in a G-string. The manager informed me that they were really impressed with my dancing and would very much like for me to come in for the second audition. On the other hand, if I could not agree on the criteria of the costume, there would be no need for me to come to the audition.

I wanted this so badly, so I conceded, went out, bought a lingerie outfit, and showed up to the audition. I was a nervous wreck to be dancing in front of people, both male and female, with my body exposed. Nevertheless, I made it through the audition and was one of four girls who made the group. I later learned at group rehearsals that the image of the background dancers was to be sexy and create a sexual illusion on stage during the group's performances.

My mom and sisters were not at all thrilled about me performing with this group. As a matter of fact, my mom had everybody at church "praying for me," and they would let me know they were praying for me whenever I went to service. My dad didn't seem to have an issue with it, and he said that he was glad I was doing something I loved to do.

After the group started performing at local clubs, they quickly received recognition as a show to attend. I quickly became comfortable with performing in the group due to the widespread attention we received. Eventually, we went on a 10-city tour throughout Texas and Louisiana with other local rap artists. Soon after, I began to choreograph skits for the background dancers, which made our stage show more exciting and generated more popularity for the background dancers. The girls of the *Sexxx Fiends* had become just as popular as the rappers, especially "Passion," who was me.

I can recall a performance at a club one night where we introduced a skit I choreographed. There was a verse in the song where one of the rappers mentions something about nuts. While he rapped that verse, in the routine, I did a backbend while he poured peanuts into my mouth. The crowd went wild, and guys rushed the stage throwing money at us. After that, we knew that we had tapped into a new level of stage performance.

As time went on, I started gaining more attention and was asked to dance in local nightclubs for tips. I hadn't been exposed to exotic dancing before except for a performance I'd seen by a group who was on tour with us. After seeing them, I secretly admired what they did and became inquisitive about dancing in night clubs, especially after I learned how well it paid, and I saw some of the girls driving nice cars. It was like what I was already doing except I was just dancing on stage and not within the crowd. When the popularity of the *Sexxx Fiends* began to simmer down and show performances became infrequent, I decided to give nightclub dancing a try. However, the attention went beyond dancing and into engaging in sexual activity with just about any guy who expressed interest in me and me in them.

The guys were too rowdy at the first club I danced at, and I decided this sort of dancing wasn't for me. However, I continued going to the clubs to party and dance socially. I made some new friends with the male and female dancers along the way and learned of some other clubs that hosted dancers. Dancing with the *Sexxx Fiends* became so infrequent that I sporadically danced in a few night clubs until the *Sexxx Fiends* era ended.

I eventually left the club scene when I became pregnant by the guy I was dating who was an aspiring rapper and we got married. This union should have been a match made in heaven with him a rapper and me a dancer. However, during our marriage, I didn't do any dancing. My husband was good looking with an infectious smile and an extremely charming personality. That was not a good mix for someone who dealt with self-esteem issues. My insecurities would always arise, and I was continuously accusing him of being with other women. He put everything into pursuing his rap career, time and money, so a family at the time just didn't fit in. He spent a lot of late hours either hanging out or in the studio; I was never invited or included in much that he did. We didn't have a bad relationship, but it wasn't the best either. We got married because "we wanted to do right by God" since I had gotten pregnant during the relationship. *Getting married due to a pregnancy birthed out of fornication is not "doing right by God."* Due to our lack of maturity, we were not ready for such a major transition in life, and therefore, the marriage didn't turn out the way we expected it would.

My life then began to take a crazy turn. I gave birth to our daughter in October, and I later finished my Associates degree with Honors from Houston Community College in December. I participated in the graduation ceremony in May of the following year, and a week later, my daddy passed away. My daddy had been in the hospital for several months for liver disease, but he was holding on to see his baby girl in her cap and gown holding my degree. He was unable to attend my graduation, but immediately following the ceremony, I went to the hospital in my cap and gown so that he could witness my accomplishment.

Soon after graduation, I was laid off from my job, and my marriage had taken a bad turn, which led me to split from my husband. Our immaturity and lack of understanding of marriage led us to not function as a married couple should have. We still did things separately, kept our money separate, and there was definitely no submission to God or to one another. Although we said getting married was to live right for God, which our marriage was not at all for God's purpose. Our immaturity led the marriage to take a nasty turn. We treated our marriage as if we were two single people living together;

you pay your bills, I'll pay mine, and we'll split the rent and food.

When he hit a financial difficulty, he had an expectation for me to help him, but he didn't know how to ask. In an effort to get himself out of his own financial crisis, he went to a casino without letting me know and stayed out all night. That is not something I felt that a married man should have done, and so out of anger, I would not let him back into our apartment when he finally arrived home. He got angry and burst through the apartment door, and a fight broke out between us. We tousled for a long time fighting one another until the unthinkable happened. He pinned me down on the floor and banged my head continuously into the floor until I thought I was going to die. He finally released me and fled when I called the police.

I know there are many women who would have taken his behavior as an indication of his frustration and thought if he wasn't in that situation, he wouldn't do it again and would have remained in the relationship. There is never, ever a reason for a man to exert such physical harm on a woman. That day, I left the apartment, I left him, and I left our marriage. I would not be a woman to stick around to see if a man would change from such behavior, or see if I'd end up being harmed more or eventually dead. He didn't take too well to my leaving, and in an effort to punish me, he cut up every article of clothing I owned including the ones in the dirty laundry. I had to start completely over. I knew I'd made the right decision to leave.

The split forced me to move back to my mom's house. My mother and I still did not get along. We had a terrible relationship, so I was hoping to make the arrangement as temporary as possible, which was difficult since I was no longer working. My husband and I eventually divorced after we were unable to reconcile the marriage even though we did consider it. I later enrolled into a Cosmetology program at another local community college in the Houston area. Not too long after, I ran into an old high school acquaintance, and he and I began talking and seeing each other on a regular basis.

Shortly thereafter, he offered for my daughter and me to move in with him and his family, and I took him up on his offer so I could get out of my mother's house. One of his sisters who lived in the home would watch my daughter during the day while I was at school. I was home with her at night while he was out with his dad and brothers working the family business. This relationship didn't last long as he quickly kicked me out of the house in a matter of a few months to make way for another female and her kids, who he'd met while out working. I learned this was a pattern for him. This left me with nowhere to go, especially not back to my mother's house. Since she urged me not to leave, my pride would not let me return. But another one of his sisters stepped up and offered to let me and my daughter stay with her and her kids in their apartment.

Purpose Principle

The emotional trauma I experienced from a failed marriage, many failed relationships, and the negative relationship I had with my mother caused me to be blinded from what was probably best for me. I was distracted by what I wanted versus yielding to what was necessary for my life at the time. I felt like I was grown, although not at a place of maturity, and so I did not want to be in my mother's home allowing her to guide me with wisdom.

Some unwise decisions made earlier in life can be contributing factors in derailing you from your purpose. Every situation we find ourselves in is a teaching moment and a place for growth and development to take place. If we are led by our feelings and emotions, we can never look past the negative to get to the positive. We most often allow ourselves to be led by our feelings and find ourselves in places or situations we were never meant to be in.

Pride is dangerous and a killer to promotion in life. You cannot be lost in your own mistakes or unwilling to move forward because you're embarrassed, ashamed, or even too stubborn to ask for direction, guidance, or instructions. But that is what God wants to do; He wants to guide you out of where you are or where you were to where He wants you to be. Even if you don't feel like it, you should let people help you; you cannot figure things out on your own. These people are who God sent to help you, and once you overcome certain challenges in your life, God wants to use you so that you can help others.

It must become essential that you do not put off acknowledging God's place in your life and His purpose for you. Do not allow your purpose to be derailed any longer than it has been. It's time to arise and allow purpose to spring forth out of the good seeds that were planted in you so that you may produce fruit that will be effective in someone else's life. If purpose has been lost, find joy in discovering it again; if purpose has been derailed, take pleasure in getting back on the right path.

⊂ꙮ Purpose Derailed ꙮ⊃

*Joseph discovered his gift from God, the interpretation of dreams. However, his discovery caused him to be placed in unfavorable positions multiple times which would make it seem like he would not reach his **purpose**. Although Joseph faced many adverse situations, he rose to fulfill his **purpose** at just the right time. (Genesis 37:5-11, 20-24, 39:20-23, 41:41,45:5, 7)*

My daughter and I moved into the apartment with my ex-friend's sister, *Pumpkin*. After being there a few days, *Pumpkin* shared with me that she danced at night at a topless bar. This was a shock to me because she had a good job as a Lab Technician. She told me how much she made in tips each night. The money sounded enticing, but this was not something I could see myself venturing into, especially after just having a baby a year prior, and my breasts had suffered because of breastfeeding. But I went on to share with her my previous dance experience with the group *Sexxx Fiends* plus my brief stint in nightclubs, and she convinced me that I could make it in the topless club world. She assured me that I would have nothing to worry about.

After giving it some thought, I called the club where she worked, *Baby Dolls*, and scheduled an interview with the manager. I went out and bought a wig and fake eye contacts to wear to disguise my identity. After meeting with the manager, he informed me that he did not have any openings for new dancers but would keep me in mind. Although the club genuinely may not have had any openings for the highway until I came across another nearby club called *Silk* where I was hired on the spot to start that evening.

I was so nervous my first night, and I hardly made any money since I was new to pole and table dancing. However, I quickly made a friend in *Paige* who showed me dancers, I took this as rejection, and because of my low self-esteem, I did not like the sense of feeling rejected. I would not settle for what I felt was rejection. Since I had finally made up my mind to venture into this new arena, I drove up and down the ropes, and I became comfortable working in the club in no time. Eventually, I learned how to hustle table dances, and because of this, a pimp who stayed in the club with a dancer he had working there tried to recruit me to join them. I refused because I already had a place to stay and my own car, and I didn't see the need to split my money with a man to provide for me what I already had.

I was a student by day and topless dancer by night. While dancing at *Silk*, a customer told me that because of my dance skills, I could probably make more money dancing at another club called *Fantasy*, which was an all nude strip club. Oh no! There was no way that I could dance totally nude in front of a bunch of strange men and women; it had already taken some time for me to become comfortable dancing topless. "Give it a try," I was told. "Start on the day shift where there are hardly any customers, and when you're ready, move to nights." I just said I would give it some thought.

Later that summer, one of my classmates was getting married, so a few of us decided to throw her a Bachelorette party and hire a male stripper. Since I was familiar with that arena, I took on the task of finding the stripper. I visited a male strip club and connected with a dancer, *Horseman*, whom I'd encountered in my past. He was one of Houston's hottest male dancers, and he also managed a group of female dancers. He was hired and performed at our mini bachelorette party, which we held on our last day of classes. After the party was over, I talked with *Horseman* about how I'd met him previously from touring with him and his girls when I danced for the *Sexxx Fiends*. He said that he remembered me and was impressed by my dancing and stage presence.

I let him know that I was currently dancing at *Silk*, and he informed me that he was having a *Player's Ball* at a local nightclub called Chocolate Town, Houston's hottest nightclub. He told me there would be plenty of female dancers and even more men eager to spend money. He invited me to come and dance although I wouldn't get paid because he'd already hired all his paid dancers, but he said I was welcomed to come join other dancers who would just be dancing for tips. Not one to pass on an opportunity to dance or make money, I accepted the invitation, especially since I didn't have to dance topless or in the nude when dancing in a nightclub.

After I agreed to perform at the *Player's Ball*, he asked what name I went by so that he could add me to the roster. I told him that I had been dancing by the name *Passion*, but he already had a Passion on the roster. So then, we were faced with the tough task of finding me a new stage name. After tossing around a few ideas, we finally found a name that we both agreed upon; I would go by the name *Capri* and later become famously known as *Lady Capri*. After giving it much thought and wanting the opportunity to make more money, I decided to go to *Fantasy* for an interview, and surely, they hired me to work days. I only went on certain days after class, and I was amongst women who were much older but still desired to work in that environment.

When it was time for the *Player's Ball*, in preparation for this big night and my debut to a new crowd in a much larger club, I went out shopping for the perfect costume. I purchased a new wig, a silver sequin dancer's outfit, which was a 3-piece set with a bikini top, G-string and shorts, and some silver boots; I was ready for this performance.

On the night of the *Player's Ball*, I arrived at the club at the appointed time. I did not know any of the girls, so I was on my own. *Horseman* was in and out of the dressing room checking on us girls as we were preparing to get ready. He then came in with a big request saying that he needed someone to open the show and asked who wanted to go first. No one volunteered. He asked again, urging us ladies by saying he needed somebody to start the show; still no response, just the girls mumbling amongst themselves. After a short while, I mustered up the courage to step forward and open the show since this was not my first time onstage. I realized that was my opportunity to introduce myself in grand fashion to a new audience. He was delighted that I volunteered.

As the show began, *Horseman* went out onto the stage and welcomed the hundreds of men who came out to the *Player's Ball*. He then announced, "We will now start the show with our first dancer. Some of you may recognize her from the group *Sexxx Fiends,* so let's welcome to the stage *Capri.*" So, I stepped up center stage to the roar of the crowd of males ready to *wow* them, and *wow* I did. The DJ played my introduction song, and I performed a stage skit to my first song selection. While dancing to my second song selection, I shed my shorts to reveal the G-string portion of my outfit before I jumped off the stage to start working the crowd by performing mini dances for tips.

That night was a huge night for me. I'd made a lot of money in tips, and by going first, I made even more because I stayed out on the floor the longest from beginning to the end of the night. This excited me even more. I was tremendously surprised to see so many black men spending money on us dancing. The response from these men was different from those in the strip clubs.

In strip clubs, in addition to dancing on stage, you had to solicit table dances at $20 a song or the private VIP room for $100. This wasn't always profitable because a lot of guys just came in to drink and watch the girls dance on stage. In the strip club, there were good money making nights and some bad. In the regular nightclubs, the guys tipped the dancer, but not all tips were ones; some guys would tip with multiple ones at a time or with five, twenty, fifty, or even a 100-dollar bill. So, that night, I found it easier to dance for tips versus table dances, and now I had a desire to dance in night club venues even more.

At the conclusion of the night, *Horseman* thanked me for coming, said he was very impressed with my performance, and noticed that I'd made plenty of money.

We kept in touch for a little while socially afterwards. Another thing that happened that night was that my dancing had gotten the attention of Chocolate Town's manager who approached me with a proposal. He stated that the club had male dancers on Sunday nights, and in the past, they had female dancers also, but they shut it down. Due to the success of the *Player's Ball*, he thought that it would be a good idea to start the female dancers again. He asked if I would come be one of the featured dancers, and he told me that the club would pay me plus I'd make tips. This overwhelmed me to think that out of all the girls that were there that night, I was the one selected to dance at the club on a regular basis and get paid by the club to do so. This was new to me because at strip clubs, you had to pay the club a fee at the end of the night known as a "tip out."

By this time, I had completed the Cosmetology program and became a licensed nail technician. Since I was done with school, I started dancing every day on the day shift at *Fantasy*. After I had gotten completely comfortable with the idea of dancing nude, I was back in my element to where my dancing skills were once again noticed. Whenever I performed in a club, although I would dance with boldness and confidence, nervousness was always present; I was especially nervous about who would walk in the club and see me onstage. There were even a few times I was embarrassed if I saw a familiar face in the audience.

Shortly after I started working more days at *Fantasy*, I quickly grabbed the attention of one of the DJ's who felt that I was much more suitable for the night shift and discussed it with the manager. I made the move to the night shift and began to make my mark with my stellar stage performances, which drew positive attention from the male customers but negative attention from the other female dancers. I only became friends with one of the dancers, and that was because she was new to the club as well.

My living arrangement with Pumpkin didn't last too long, only about a couple of months, following a dispute between us. So, once again, I moved back to my mother's house until I could get my own apartment. Refusing to give up my *night gig* or even let my mother know what I was doing, I told her that I was working at Wal-Mart at night as a stocker so she would agree to watch my daughter. To push this lie even further, I met a customer in the club who worked at Wal-Mart, and he gave me a vest and stocking belt, which I kept in my car to keep up the deception.

I danced several nights during the week, mainly on weekends, to gain customers and make more money so that I could save money to move into my own apartment. I was also making enemies amongst the other dancers, especially when I "stole" one of their regular customers for a table dance. Eventually, things got so heated between me and a couple of the other girls at *Fantasy* that they ended up running me off from the club. I then moved on to working at "high profile" topless clubs. I went to these clubs thinking I could meet a millionaire and possibly become the next *Anna Nicole*, just as so many other female dancers did. Because the entire clientele of these clubs was of a different race than me, I just didn't mesh well in that environment. So, I bounced around to various topless and nude clubs until I decided to quit these clubs altogether.

I eventually started dancing at the nightclub *Chocolate Town* on a Sunday night with another girl whom I was unfamiliar with. The dance time was cut short that night because the guys had gotten pretty rowdy soon after we started dancing from the excitement of having female dancers again. I gave it another try the following three weeks. Each week, the crowd of males grew larger, and eventually another dancer was added. But the crowd had grown so much to where it had gotten too out of control, so I threatened to quit. The set up was that the females danced in a small area at the back of the club while the males danced on the main dance floor at the front of the club. The club's owner and manager came up with the idea to move the females to the front of the club at an earlier time on Sunday nights, and we would clear out once it was time for the male dancers to perform during their regularly scheduled time. This new arrangement worked out very well as the crowd of male patrons grew week after week. We even began adding more girls, and I became the lead over all the girls. I was responsible for organizing the performance line up of the female dancers, of which I always danced first along with one or two others whom I selected to open the show with me.

The popularity of the female dance show at this club grew throughout the city drawing patrons from all over – the show was announced weekly on the radio and the DJ encouraged guys to come out to see the featured dancers *Lady Capri, Tasty, Seduction, Temptation, and Ice.* There were other girls, but we were the featured dancers of the club;

there were even flyers of us and our show passed around the city week after week.

On one Saturday night, *Chocolate Town* had a special Male Dance Revue where they invited the Chippendale Dancers from Atlanta to perform. After the show was over, I had gotten the chance to meet the dancers and spent some time with one of them at their hotel. The meeting time with him helped to take my dance performance to a whole new level. He told me about how the girls at the clubs in Atlanta performed and that I had to come up with a skit that would make me a dancing sensation. After tossing around a few suggestions and ideas, he finally told me about one I thought would be suitable for me to perform.

It was Easter Sunday of 1997; I introduced my new skit to the male crowd of *Chocolate Town*. I was dressed in an all-white, velour halter top G-string one-piece, white boots, and bunny ears, and I had an Easter basket filled with candy. I stepped out onto the dance floor. During the dancer's performances, the club manager always gave commentary to keep the crowd hyped. As I was setting up, he, along with the other guys in the club, anticipated what I was up to and gave commentary of my actions. I set up a white plush rug in the center of the dance floor where I placed and lit 4 candles with one in each corner of the rug. I danced to my intro song passing out candy as the candles burned.

When I saw the wax melted, I danced down onto the rug, grab the candles one by one and poured the candle wax all over my body. The crowd roared in amazement, and the males rushed to the dance floor throwing money at me. This new skit created a lot of buzz about me, and my popularity grew even more throughout the Houston club scene. This resulted in other small to medium sized night clubs adding female dancers on different nights of the week, and I was hired as the paid featured dancer. I performed my new skit everywhere I went; my skit and I continued to grow in popularity, thus growing the crowds of every club I performed in. I was also constantly getting booked for bachelor parties and private parties where my "candle wax" skit was always the highlight of the night. The performance of this skit always gained me tips in excess amounts.

Purpose Principle

Not knowing your purpose can cause you to negatively affect someone else's life to the point where they would get off the path leading to their own purpose. Since my roommate apparently didn't know her life's purpose at the time, and neither did I know mine, I allowed her lack of knowing who she really was to affect me. When I made the decision to follow her influence, I set myself up to go in an entirely different direction than what was meant for my life.

The direction in which I had gone fully derailed me from where I was supposed to have been at this point in my life. I didn't even recognize the road that I was on while trying to get to where my heart desired. I didn't see that I had gone to a place that I wasn't supposed to be, that had taken me further than I wanted to go, and would eventually leave me longer than I should have stayed. I wouldn't say that this road I was on was a rough one, but it wasn't easy either. I was nothing like the person people saw in the clubs. I was really out of my element; I was an introvert living in the shell of low self-esteem and rejection, but the club scene gave me the chance to be someone I normally wasn't — desirable, popular, and almost famous.

The paths that we travel, whether right or wrong, will always yield fruit, whether good or bad. We can determine the fruit that our lives will produce by the direction in which we take our lives; we decide whether we yield to what we want to do or yield to what we should be doing. We must take the opportunity to find the purpose, plan, and direction for our lives versus living according to our own will and desires. The paths we travel will always have some form of obstacles. Yes, there are challenges when we are on the right road to our purpose; however, when you're on the wrong road that's leading you away from purpose, the challenges can be even greater.

Wrong turns off the path to purpose can deter you from reaching your proposed destination. Not only do we allow our own actions to take us down wrong paths, but we also do so in our thoughts. The mind is the starting point of leading you down the wrong path. You must have control over your thinking and keep your thoughts focused on Christ. The path that we're traveling can be a smooth or rocky one; it can take us uphill and definitely downhill. It can also be filled with the highs and lows of life, as well as bring us joy and pain. Purpose can be aimless when you are trying to find your own way or do things your own way. When you are doing things outside of God's way, you are sure to get off the path that leads to His promise and end up on a path of destruction. The path that you choose will always lead you further away from your purposed destination and leave you longer than you were meant to stay.

When we are outside the will of purpose and the will of God, the struggle to get back can be even more challenging. "There is a way which seems right to a man, but its end is the way of death" (Proverbs 14:12). If you are not living in purpose, there must be a willingness and determination to do so. If you've taken a path in your life that is not leading you in a positive, purposeful, or productive direction, I encourage you to make a U-turn and head in the other direction. Let's get your life on the path that will lead to God's purpose and plan for you because your destiny awaits you.

☙ The Divine Set-up ❧

*Saul was a brutal man who brought about great persecution, threat
and murder to the saints of the church. In the midst of his
wrongdoings, Jesus seized him from his plan to be a chosen vessel
with the **purpose** of making him a minister and witness of Christ.
(Acts 9:1, 10-16, 26:16).*

While I was in Cosmetology school, we received visits
from local hair and nail salon owners to evaluate the
students as well as select students to be potential employees.
A nail salon owner who was evaluating me at the time
expressed a great interest in me as she was impressed with
my work, and she told me that after I passed my state board,
I would have a job at her salon. A visit to her nail salon a
short time afterwards made me excited with anticipation to
be able to work there. However, an employee greeted me
with negativity about the salon and the owner, which
brought about disappointment, so I opted out of taking a job
there.

Nonetheless, a short time after that visit, an
appointment at a hair salon led to a promising second
opportunity. As I was getting my hair done, I was telling the
stylist, who happened to be the salon owner, that I'd just
became a licensed nail technician. She was thrilled at hearing
this because she was moving into a new larger salon that
would have a nail station. I was invited to return to perform
nail services on a model as part of the interview process. I

did return, and she was pleased with my skills and extended an offer for me to rent the nail booth in her new salon. I started working in the new salon, *New Age Hair Salon*, by day while I still danced in nightclubs at night.

At this point, I was getting booked to travel and perform at nightclubs, events, and private parties out of town. I had also connected with other dancers with whom I became friends with, and we danced at clubs and parties together. There were two dancers I hung with the most. One went by the name *Motor Booty*, and we lived in the same apartment complex, and the other went by the name *Satin*. I was now living in my own two bedrooms, two bath apartment, in which *Motor Booty* helped me to secure. Since she had already been living in the complex, she was cool with the manager, and I was able to rent an apartment without having to show proof of income.

Motor Booty and I danced mostly together at private parties, and *Satin* and I danced together at various clubs. I met them both at a club where we all happened to be dancing for a special party that night. *Motor Booty* noticed how I was a "go-getter" dancer who knew how to make my money, and she liked that. She was a proclaimed bi-sexual dancer. There were a lot of female dancers who were either gay or bi-sexual; since I was neither, *Motor Booty* became my protector by not allowing anyone to mess with me. She and I danced together sporadically at clubs because she didn't really like the club guys. So, her main thing was private parties because that was where she made the most money.

When dancing in clubs, guys would whisper in a dancer's ear, "Do you date?" This meant do you have sex for money. When guys were interested in private and bachelor parties, they asked, "Do you trick?" This was also another term for having sex for money. Whenever I booked private parties, my response would be, "No," but I would let the person know that I could bring someone with me who did. That is not something that I did, but I knew *Motor Booty* and another dancer named *Pleasure* did those activities. I tried it before, but I didn't like it since it seemed liked prostitution; I decided that was not an activity that I wanted to be involved in. For those parties where such activity was requested, I would call either *Motor Booty* or *Pleasure*, and let them know that I had booked a private party. I asked if they wanted to come along, letting them know that they wouldn't get paid for dancing, but they could make their money the other way, and they always agreed. It was a good thing I befriended these ladies because sex after the dancers performed was highly anticipated (especially for Bachelor parties), and I didn't want to be a participant. The most I would do was give a guy a hand job and charge them for it.

I was dancing in night clubs every night of the week except for Saturday nights, which were reserved for private parties and special events. At this point, dancing had become a fulltime job for me, and I was making enough money to fully sustain my livelihood. I wasn't making much money in the salon doing nails as it was hard at the time for a new black nail technician to gain confidence with black women when they were accustomed to the Vietnamese nail salons, so it was good that the dancing was financially lucrative.

I was also dating a guy who was a drug dealer in his town, so he would pay my rent and give me money. Dating drug dealers was a norm for me. I dated guys who had the money and the capability to do things for me, such as pay my rent, car note, get my hair or nails done, or buy me things. I never received anything extravagant from these guys or lived a luxurious life, but whatever they would do for me was fine by me as long as they were doing something.

My popularity around the city's club scene grew. I'd become kind of a local celebrity with my name being announced on the radio for clubs that I'd been featured at and with my picture on flyers. When I went to clubs socially and the DJ saw me, I'd be announced as being in the building and receive plenty attention from the male club goers. The female dancers were so popular on Sunday nights at *Chocolate Town* that every Sunday after we danced, a few of us took pictures with the guys by a photographer who was setup at the back of the club. The photographer charged $5 for the picture and the dancers charged a $5 tip to be in the picture with them. For the remainder of the night after dancing, my time was spent taking pictures until closing time; this was week after week for months.

One of my main motivations for dancing in these clubs was for the recognition and, of course, the attention. Oftentimes, dancers in nightclubs and strip clubs were discovered by artists, record company executives, or personnel. I was just biding my time waiting for my opportunity to come.

Then, it finally happened; I got my opportunity to be in a rap music video. This was the moment I'd been waiting years for; my self-proclaimed purpose was finally coming to fruition. *Motor Booty* was going to an audition for a video shoot for a very popular rap group, and she asked me for a ride. While we were at the location of the audition, I was suddenly recognized and invited to audition as well, which I enthusiastically obliged. Following the audition, I was invited to the video shoot days later; I was so excited to finally get my opportunity to dance in a rap music video. However, this was not the hip hop dance video that I'd dreamed that I would be in. Yes, it was for a rap group, but the song for this video was one that represented women in a "sexy" manner. The required costume for the girls for this video shoot was a lingerie dress. At this point, I was no longer bothered by the attire since that's what I'd been accustomed to wearing, so I went out and purchased the perfect ensemble; a black see-thru mesh dress that stopped mid-thigh with hot pink fur around the top bodice and bottom hem.

When my friend and I showed up to the video set bright and early on the morning of the shoot, there were over 30 other girls there. This was not expected. After wondering why there were so many girls, we were then told that one of the scenes would be set up as a large party scene for a guest rap artist making a feature in the video. The rap group had three rappers who would be shooting solo scenes, each with a feature girl. Each of the 30 girls was looked over thoroughly to choose the feature girls. Surprisingly, I was one of the three chosen. Here was now my chance to shine.

After the introduction and party scenes were shot, everyone else was released, and we began shooting the feature scenes. The feature scenes were each filmed in a different bedroom of the mansion used for the video, with only the rapper and feature girl in their individual scenes.

Whenever I danced, I always gave my best, but this time I had to make sure that my dance performance was great. While dancing in the clubs, I learned to not only dance to the words of the song but to the beat as well. For the part of the song I was featured in, there was a very distinctive and unique beat. I executed dance movements, especially with my booty, precisely to that particular beat, which amazed the manager and crew; even the rapper was impressed once he saw the video playback.

The video was going to be shown on BET's regular video programing, but they were also shooting for BET After Dark and separate video sales. We were asked by the group's manager if we would shoot scenes for the uncut version for additional pay. Reluctantly, I agreed, but only if they would allow me to dance without showing my face, and they agreed. The video shoot was long, over 16 hours of filming, and had gone late into the evening.

After the video was released, played on television, and video tapes were sold, people started recognizing me and asked, "Are you the girl in the video?" to which my response was a shy, "Yes." I was told that it was the way I danced that made me stand out from amongst the other feature girls. Although this was what I wanted, the recognition was almost embarrassing, because of the song, especially from those around my college campus. After the word spread about my feature in the video, more men flocked to the clubs to see me perform in person, and they especially came on Sunday's to *Chocolate Town* to have their picture taken with me; I was even signing autographs.

Purpose Principle

Although I was fully engrossed in my lifestyle as a stripper, as I continued on that path, it was revealed to me exactly what was happening. My life had now begun taking a path of its own as I thought this was exactly what I wanted to be doing. I never looked at it as if I was degrading myself or discounting my value or worth by the things I was doing. The attention, the fame, and the almost celebrity-like status was more fulfilling to me than I was to myself. I valued all the attention, although degrading, over valuing myself as a person.

Purpose is not something that can be avoided, especially if you are connected to the power source: God. Your purpose is not only important for you, but it is the answer needed to solve problems in the lives of others. God created us as problem solvers. The world is full of problems and so are the people of the world. "The Spirit of the Lord is upon Me, Because He has anointed Me to preach the gospel to the poor; He has sent Me to heal the brokenhearted, to proclaim liberty to the captives And recovery of sight to the blind, to set at liberty those who are oppressed; to proclaim the acceptable year of the Lord" (Luke 4:18-19). You are supposed to be making a difference in the world; there is something in this world that you were put here to do and only you can do it. The answer lies within you and is revealed through your purpose. There is potential within you that you must cultivate and impart to others, just as the mission of Jesus was to come give life to a hurting world. "Yes, I am the gate. Those who come in through me will be saved. They will come and go freely and will find good pastures. The thief's purpose is to steal and kill and destroy. My purpose is to give them a rich and satisfying life," (John 10:9-10 NLT).

When God created mankind, He created us for Himself (Isaiah 43:7). That purpose and plan has not gone away. If you are living outside of your purpose and outside of God's will for your life, how can you positively affect, impact, or even inspire other people who you encounter? God's basis for humanity is to use people to carry out His will on earth to reconcile and restore people back to Him. Your purpose is to help someone else who needs to overcome the challenges they are faced with in life and help those who are not living a life that is pleasing to God to come out of how they are living. This is the demonstration of the love of God, and it honors God when you allow Him to show up through you. "Blessed be the God and Father of our Lord Jesus Christ, the Father of mercies and God of all comfort, who comforts us in all our tribulation, that we may be able to comfort those who are in any trouble, with the comfort with which we ourselves are comforted by God," (2 Corinthians 1:3-4).

CS The Divine Intervention *SO*

*When Pharaoh would not let the children of Israel go so that they may serve God, He sent many plagues upon the house of Pharaoh. God **purpose** for Moses was to call forth the plagues upon Pharaoh and the land of Egypt so that His name would be proclaimed and glorified in all the earth. (Exodus 9:16)*

At the New Age salon, I quickly became good friends with one of the hairstylist, Genell, who is still my lifelong best friend and sister. She was a small girl with a very large personality, and she always made her presence known. Many of the other stylists in the salon couldn't handle her personality, mainly because she often used bad language. That was something I had come to overlook because of her always positive attitude and the inspirational and encouraging things she would speak. It was the word of God. One thing she would continuously profess is her love for God, and she always shared the messages she heard at church.

I was drawn to the things I'd heard her speaking about. Although I had been going to the church of my youth, now sporadically because of my "night job," I had never heard the things she spoke of. By her continuously sharing the Word in the salon, she was sowing a spiritual seed into me. I know there are many who would probably argue that there is no way a person who uses bad language could effectively speak the word of God. From personal experience, I beg to differ. Yes, she cursed and did so quite often, but when she spoke the word, it was profound and there was power in it. I am a living witness and testimony of it.

Genell was familiar with my night life. Since we were friends, she was the only one in the salon with whom I shared my personal information with. She also saw me dance when she came to one of my performances. She did not pass judgment against me or treat me any differently; she continued to be herself and let the love of God flow through her as she continued to share the Word with me as she always had. She truly exemplified 1 Corinthians 9:19-23 MSG *"Even though I am free of the demands and expectations of everyone, I have voluntarily become a servant to any and all in order to reach a wide range of people: religious, nonreligious, meticulous moralists, loose-living immoralists, the defeated, the demoralized—whoever. I didn't take on their way of life. I kept my bearings in Christ—but I entered their world and tried to experience things from their point of view. I've become just about every sort of servant there is in my attempts to lead those I meet into a God-saved life. I did all this because of the Message. I didn't just want to talk about it; I wanted to be in on it!"*

As a result, in March of 1998, I approached her and asked if I could go to church with her, and she excitedly said "Yes." Several weeks later, I met her at New Light Christian Center church. I was very late and had to sit in an overflow area. I was very moved by the sermon from the Pastor. I was even more amazed at how the Pastor was showing us the scriptures in the bible pertaining to everything that he was teaching about; I'd never seen such a thing. The sermon was exactly how my friend would share information each week in the salon. I returned to church the next week for Easter Sunday. I arrived on time and got to experience Praise & Worship for the first time; the entire service was amazing. I knew that would not be my last time visiting this church. So, the seeds that had been sown into me were now being watered by my continued visits to that church. As time passed, I ended up leaving the salon to get another job working during the day. I started working for a temporary agency on assignments in the corporate arena by day. I was still dancing in the clubs at night while taking classes at Texas Southern University and raising my daughter.

After dancing in my first music video, I now had a new goal. The rapper Master P was out and hot on the charts, and my goal was to dance in one of his music videos. My life was moving at a fast pace as I was working, going to school, dancing, and now doing videos. I'd also began working with a record label in Dallas where I danced in the clubs there, and I organized girls for club events and calendar photo shoots. In addition to all that I was doing, I'd begun to go to the new church more often.

About a month after my first video, I received a call from the video director stating there were two video shoots coming up, and I was requested to be one of the feature girls. One of the videos was for a local Houston rapper and another from New Orleans, who just happened to be on Master P's record label. I thought surely this was my chance at getting closer to being in one of Master P's music videos. *Motor Booty* and I attended both video shoots together, which were on the same day, and that turned out to be another long night with over 12 hours of shooting. The first video featured me dancing in various scenes with the artist. In the second video, I wasn't a feature girl as there were numerous girls grouped together dancing in various scenes. After the shoot was over, I was approached by the rapper, and he expressed that he wanted me to be featured in the uncut version of the video where there would be only three girls dancing in various scenes. I agreed with stipulations of extra pay and not showing my face, which they agreed with. The rapper even gave me his baseball cap for me to wear to help conceal my identity. I still had anticipation that once Master P saw this video, surely, I would be getting a call to be invited to dance in his next music video. However, the opportunity never came.

At the time, I was also working on a new business plan to make my dance career more profitable. During the times that I was being hired for private parties directly, I had the task of recruiting other dancers to come along. I came up with a plan to slowly phase myself out of dancing and just manage the dancers who would be mostly young girls younger than me who were runaways or homeless. I'd gotten this idea from one of my rapper friends, because this was something that he'd started doing. Sometimes, I took his girls to clubs with me so they could work, and he'd give me a cut. I knew others who managed girls as well. I was making serious preparations to get out of performing and move to the management side of dancing. I'd also had the idea to open my own club. Consequently, these plans never came to fruition.

I was attending Sunday services at New Light Christian Center church regularly, and the seed of redemption was continuously being watered. I was praying more and even giving tithes and offerings. Yes, I was putting 10% of my dancing money in the offering envelopes along with my tithe from my paycheck. I'd begun to have faith in the tithe principle that I'd heard taught, and the money I made from dancing was increase. I truly believed that my giving during this stage in my life not only set me up to where I am now, fully committed to the things of God, but it also protected me. I also believe with my whole heart that God had his hand and a hedge of protection around me throughout this period in my life after I'd begun attending services at New Light. I believe God was protecting His call and purpose for my life.

I feel this way because there were many times when I was in what seemed to have been some very dangerous predicaments, yet nothing ever happened to me. I would go to dance at private parties either solo or with other dancers for guys we knew nothing about and had often just met. These parties either took place in apartments, homes, or hotel rooms. I even danced for guys privately in my own apartment. I also traveled out of town to dance at private parties in clubs, homes, or hotels for people whom I'd never previously met. Private parties were usually booked by someone seeing you dancing in a club or at another private party, from people who managed dancers, or based off referrals. I knew of other female dancers who were robbed, beaten, raped, and even killed. I never once in all my years of dancing experienced any hardships or bad things happening to me. I believe this was all by the grace of God.

The only thing I've ever experienced is a guy who I was supposedly dating and working for, the owner of the record label, take advantage of me by getting money from me for business investments in which I never received a return on. A couple of times he even left me stranded when I would travel to Dallas to visit him or to dance. I later found out he was married and wasn't the business person he'd made himself out to be. Now that I think back to all those predicaments I had been in, I am petrified and disturbed that I'd done such things. I thank God I survived it all.

Purpose Principle

Getting the job in this particular hair salon was truly a setup for the turning point in my life that I didn't initially recognize. Since New Age Salon was not the place that I originally was supposed to work at, I could question, "How did I get there?" Have you ever found yourself in a place where you're not quite sure how you got there? Well, God knew you were going to be there, and he had the perfect plan in place for you to meet your purpose in that place and to lead you to your destiny. My working in this salon where one of the hairstylists was a Christian, who unashamedly and boldly spoke the word of God, was God intervening in my life. He used Genell to get me off the road of destruction that I was on and onto the path He had for my life. That is why I called the previous chapter The Divine Setup because working there was surely God's intervention in my life.

Your life was designed to be a sacrifice to God. "Therefore, I urge you, brothers and sisters, in view of God's mercy, to offer your bodies as a living sacrifice, holy and pleasing to God—this is your true and proper worship" (Romans 12:1 NIV). God can only operate in the earth through a person, and the purpose for your life was designed to be used by God when there is something that He wants fulfilled on Earth. Presenting yourself as a sacrifice unto God by identifying and operating in your purpose gives God permission to use you for His will to be fulfilled. Since we exist for the benefit of others, your unique gift, talent, skill, or ability is to be effective in the life of another; this leads to the fulfillment of purpose. There must be a willingness and desire to offer up yourself to be used by God as He sees fit.

There are many ways in which God can use you to make a difference; you just have to be willing to yield your gift, passion, or even tragedy to Him. Just as my friend whose passion and occupation of doing hair used her gift to spread the word of God to me. God can use a hairstylist to listen to the cares, concerns, and issues of their clients and prompt them to share a word to encourage and inspire that person to show His love and compassion for those who are in need. God expects for us to love as He loves and have compassion for others as He does. "A certain man went down from Jerusalem to Jericho, and fell among thieves, who stripped him of his clothing, wounded him, and departed, leaving him half dead. But a certain Samaritan, as he journeyed, came where he was. And when he saw him, he had compassion…'Go and do likewise'" (Luke 10:30, 36-37).

Being sensitive to the spirit of God and obeying His prompting is key to walking in purpose. God wants to give you instructions to impart into others. He wants to reveal His purpose for you, and it is associated with your gift, skill, or even in your occupation.

God does not want anyone to be lost, hurt, broken, bitter, angry, resentful, unfulfilled, burdened, or abused. God wants everyone to be healed, whole, fruitful, fulfilled, and living the abundant life. For those who are not living fruitful and fulfilled lives, God is not pleased, and because He wants your life to be so, He is going to use others to help encourage and comfort you so that you can live the life God has for you. God wants to do the same through you and that is why your purpose in life is vitally important.

⚝ The Divine Revelation ⚟

*When the Pharisees brought an adulterous woman to Jesus, Jesus did not condemn her. This woman's sins were used for the **purpose** of enlightening them of their own self convictions. (John 8:3-11)*

A few of the females I danced with on a regular basis were in their late 30s or early 40s; at the time, *Motor Booty* was 38, *Honey* was 40, and *Pleasure* was 42. They all had school-aged children who knew what their mothers did for a living. My daughter was close to turning 3 years old, and I was 25. Although I was still young, I began to think that I did not want to be a 40-year-old dancer; surely, this is not how I want my daughter to know me. I wanted to make a change for the sake of my daughter and her future.

Now that I was attending a church that taught the Word of God, not only did I look at church differently, but I also looked at life differently. I started to have a new mindset, and begun having thoughts about how my life should be worth a lot more than dancing for men in clubs and at parties for a bunch of lustful men. Never once did I think that my youthful desire to be a background dancer in music videos and on award shows, a crave for attention, quest for success, and eagerness for fame would lead me here. I truly was blinded by my own ambition. This was not the life I was born to live.

On Father's Day in June of 1998, I went to church that Sunday morning. When I went to the club that night, I knew it would be my last night. I told the manager that I was giving up dancing to give my life to the Lord. Of course, he said I was making a big mistake, but he wished me the best. Once it was time for us to dance, the manager announced that this would be my farewell show. I think I took more pictures that night than in all the time I'd been there. I probably shouldn't have taken pictures that night knowing that I was leaving to give my life to the Lord, and I should not have left that memory of me with those guys.

A seed was planted in me by my friend from the salon, and the seed was watered every time she talked about the word and when I visited at her church, and now, God was giving the increase (1 Corinthians 3:6-7). God had gotten me exactly where He wanted me so that He could reach my heart and get my life back to Him. Although I was still dancing sporadically at other clubs during the week, especially on Friday nights, and performing at private parties, I began praying to God, "God, if you give me a job at night I will completely quit dancing." God heard my prayer.

Working with the temp agency, we got paid every Friday and normally I would just have the recruiter mail my check to me. On one particular Friday, I decided to pick up my check from the office. Before I left, I was led to ask the recruiter if she had any positions at night, and she responded with a resounding "Yes." She was currently in the process of sending candidates for interviews at a company that worked night shifts 6p-11p and until midnight on Fridays. I told her sign me up, and I went for the interview.

I went to the company, a check processing center, interviewed with the supervisor, and took the required test for the position. I did not pass the test, which disappointed me. Surely, I thought this would be my way out of dancing. **But God!** The supervisor told me that he would create another position for me because he felt I would be a good fit for his team. God had answered my prayer. He created a processing clerk position for me, and the next day, I started working at my new night job. Since it was at night, I could no longer dance in the clubs like I had. I tried to continue to dance on Friday's at the nightclub I traveled out of town to, but that didn't work because most Friday nights we got off close to midnight or later. However, I still danced at private parties on Saturday nights.

Purpose Principle

How I started to view those older dancers was a revelation for me of how I did not want my life to be at their age, and so I began to think differently about my life and my daughter's future. My new outlook caused me to be proactive in making purposeful changes to my life. My friend's life had been impacted by the Word of God, and she was unashamed about sharing it with others. "For I am not ashamed of the gospel of Christ: for it is the power of God unto salvation to everyone that believes..." (Romans 1:16). Had she been ashamed of her life in Christ and not spoke up about the goodness of God in her life so openly in the hair salon, my life would not have been impacted in the way it was. I would not have been led to true salvation when I needed it most. When you live your life for Christ and it has caused you walk in a new character, you should readily share it with others.

God has given you a voice to declare and share His love and goodness; therefore, use your voice to share your life's situations and how God brought you through them. You may have gone through some things in life that you think may not qualify you to share the word of God, but your life's story is important. The things you've gone through may be designed to help someone else not go through the same struggles or make the same mistakes. Your life's story may be connected to someone's deliverance. Others can be freed and grow from the testimony of your life and be encouraged to move past their own mistakes. Victory testimonies are motivators because you were born to make an impact; you must strive to walk in the purpose that your victory has developed. Positive and influential impartation in someone else's life helps to develop them to do the same for others. "But indeed, for this purpose I have raised you up; that I may show My power in you, and that my name may be declared in all the earth" (Exodus 9:16).

⟡ The Call to Purpose ⟡

*Jesus met and talked to the Samaritan woman at the well and told her all things. She believed on him and told others about him. This meeting of the Samaritan woman and Jesus was orchestrated with the **purpose** of her hearing the word, believing it, receiving it and then sharing with others so that they too may believe.*
(John 4:7-26, 39-42)

On Sunday, July 18, 1998, after the ministering of the word, the preacher extended the invitation for salvation, the baptism of Holy Spirit, and church membership. I heard God speak two simple words to my heart; "It's time." I knew exactly what it meant. That day, I accepted the call to live in my **eternal** purpose, and live my life for the Lord Jesus Christ. I was ministered to for salvation, was filled with the Holy Spirit, and became a full member of New Light Christian Center church. My dancing days were over. I went from making up to $4,000 or more a week to making less than $2,000 a month. It was now time for me to trust God with every single area of my life, and I had to make lifestyle adjustments to fit my new lower income. I continued to work two jobs, but I downsized to a one bedroom apartment.

As Christmas approached, I thought it would be difficult for me to buy my daughter Christmas gifts because of my decreased income. After paying tithes and offerings, I had to squeeze rent, car note, insurance, utilities, and food out of my now small paycheck with hardly anything left over. I hadn't gotten rid of my dance garments yet, so I called up one of my old dance friends *Satin*, who I used to travel with on Friday nights to a club out of town. When I danced at this club on Friday nights, it was one of the places where I made the most money besides private parties. The club was in a small town called Port Arthur, the home of *UGK*, and the guys were always excited to have some of Houston's hottest dancers at the club. I told *Satin* that I wanted to tag along with her that Friday. Knowing that I was now saved, she asked, "Are you sure that's what you want to do?" I really didn't want to, but my excuse was that I really needed the money to be able to buy my daughter Christmas gifts. A guy from church who I talked to on a regular basis knew of my past life as a dancer, and I told him of my plans to go to the club to try and make some money for Christmas gifts. He tried to persuade me not to go and told me that, "God would provide," but being a babe in Christ, I wasn't fully convinced of that just yet.

From the moment I got into *Satin's* car, the Holy Spirit tugged at my heart persuading me not to go through with what I was planning to do. I felt the Holy Spirit pulling at me all throughout the 90-minute drive until we arrived at the club and started dancing. The Spirit of God was urging me to turn around, but I ignored Him. A lot of the guys were thrilled to see me back. When one of my regular customers asked where I had been, I told him "I got saved," and he immediately pushed me away from dancing for him. He put money in my hand, told me that I should not be doing this, and told me not to come back. I moved on from him and went to dance for other men throughout the club, but no one gave me much money. This was crazy because I always received plenty of money from the guys in this club. Feeling defeated, I eventually stopped dancing as it seemed like the money was not flowing that night even though the club was packed. Finally, I got dressed, sat at the bar, and talked with a few guys while I waited for the night to end.

When we got into the car to leave, I told *Satin*, "Tonight was slow I think I hardly made any money, and no one was spending," but her response to me was that she had made plenty of money. That night, I made a measly $65, which was nothing compared to the hundreds of dollars I used to make from this club. I was very disappointed with myself. I felt my lack of financial productivity that night was God's way of showing me to never go against His spirit. I repented. That was my very last time dancing, and I never looked back.

On my night job, I excelled in my position as a clerk, and the supervisor allowed me to be a backup for the position that I originally interviewed for. After learning the role and excelling, I was offered the position which came with higher pay. I was able to bring my dance friend *Satin* into the company to fill my newly vacated position. I led her to give her life to Christ and leave dancing.

Purpose Principle

The journey towards my self-defined purpose led me to make many dumb decisions where I went places that I should not have gone, fraternized with people that I should not have, and exposed myself to things that had no place in my life. When we do these types of things, we open ourselves up to demonic forces and allow them to encroach upon our lives. When we are born again through Christ Jesus, those spiritual forces intensify, and we are led into a spiritual warfare. We have to work hard to uproot all that we were exposed to so that we may live a spirit-filled life. Self-defined purposes are clearly outside of the will and purpose of God. "There is a way that seems right to a man, but its end is the way of death. The person who labors, labors for himself..." (Proverbs 16:25-26).

Releasing myself from my self-proclaimed purpose and receiving my eternal purpose was important for my life. "That whoever believes in Him should not perish but have eternal life." (John 3:15). In doing so, I gained understanding of the familiar and perverse spirits that were affecting my life and keeping me from God's purpose and destiny for my life. The enemy to purpose knew that God had a plan for my life, and he was working to try and keep me from it by keeping me in bondage to a lifestyle of perversion.

Apart from dancing, I no longer had a positive self-image, and my low self-esteem was now magnified. I was influenced by seducing spirits during my dancing days, and that spirit did not leave me alone when I got saved. My now saved self still knew how to attract men with my body, and the spirit of lust kept me in the familiar place of fornication. My spirit got saved, but my flesh didn't. I still had fleshly issues that I didn't realized I needed to work on.

A critical element to moving forward towards our purpose is to identify if there are any familiar spirits that are lingering around influencing our behavior. It is important to take authority and remove these spirits from your life to receive deliverance and healing so that you may live in freedom. "Therefore, if the Son makes you free, you shall be free indeed" (John 8:36). It doesn't matter where you come from; your life has a purpose in the plan of God. "Therefore, if anyone is in Christ, he is a new creation; old things have passed away; behold, all things have become new" (2 Corinthians 5:17). Neither your environment nor your past can negate the purpose of God for your life; God is not limited or moved by your past and neither should you. "Do not remember the former things, nor consider the things of old. Behold, I will do a new thing, now it shall spring forth…" (Isaiah 43:18-19). But when you get saved, your freedom is not necessarily automatic; you must work at it and get others to help you. Be accountable to someone and receive true deliverance.

God will use a vessel that is willing to hear, obey, and share His goodness. You are a gem who cannot remain hidden within the minefield of yourself. Allow the purpose of God to be uncovered in you so that you can be used in a mighty way. God's purpose for you is not about you. Coming to the realization of this will propel your release of purpose into what God wants to do through you. "…Forgetting the past and looking forward to what lies ahead, press on to reach the end of the race and receive the heavenly prize for which God, through Christ Jesus, is calling us." (Philippians 3:13-14 NIV).

☞ The Call to Ministry ☜

Moreover, whom He predestined, these He also called; whom He called, these He also justified; and whom He justified, these He also glorified. (Romans 8:30)

I did everything you are supposed to do as a new Christian; I was reading and studying my bible, telling people about my new life, and I was always at church for every service and special event. It's funny how when I was in the clubs, people were praying for me to get out. However, when I got into church and people asked, "What are you doing today or this weekend?" and my response would be, "Going to church." Their reaction would be, "You're going to church again?" Well, where else should I be going? Back then, I wanted to get a more in-depth study of the word, so I went to Bible College. I completed four certificate programs and became a licensed minister. During this time, I even got engaged to a guy who was a Prophet; unfortunately, the relationship didn't last. Little did I know, this was the beginning of preparations for me to be in ministry and the calling God had for my life, which I learned many years later.

Although I knew I had a gift and talent to dance, I felt that dancing was over for me when I stopped in 1998. Several years later, I learned about praise dance. At the time, I had never seen it because my church at the time did not have it in the ministry. I started searching the internet and took an interest. Not too long thereafter, a praise dance ministry was started in my church, and when open auditions were held, I auditioned. I was not selected and that crushed me, so I gave up the idea of ever dancing again.

In preparation for my wedding in June of 2004, I wanted to do a special presentation for my groom. Although I'd never done it before, my sister suggested that I create a praise dance and record it. I selected the song "*More Than What I Wanted*" by CeCe Winans, and my sister helped me choreograph moves to the song. My videographer and I went to the exact place where my husband proposed, and we recorded my dance. It was edited like a music video and was presented on our wedding day. I moved to Delaware after my wedding, and upon showing our wedding video to a few church members, one being the dance ministry leader, she stated that I should join their dance team, but I didn't readily accept.

On November 19, 2004, I went to a women's meeting at a church in Philadelphia, PA, and prior to the ministering of the word, there was ministry in dance. I was so mesmerized by the dance and the graceful movements of the dancer; it was like nothing I'd ever seen before. During the ministry of dance, God spoke to me and said this is what I am calling you to do. He literally orchestrated my path to dance ministry from that moment forth. Moments later, the dancer came and sat next to me, and God told me to ask her for her phone number. After service ended, I nervously told her that I would like to speak to her about dance and asked for her phone number, which she excitedly obliged. From that day forward, I set out to learn what I could about praise dance. I gave her a call, but when I learned that she was a Pastor, Pastor Yvette Gaines, I quickly backed out and did not leave a message or try to contact her again.

A month later, I enrolled in a Praise Dance class at the local Cultural Arts Center in my town. However, after a couple of months into the class, I realized I was not getting what I was looking for because I was not learning anything about what it meant to praise dance. All we were learning was dance choreography, which was outstanding as I had a phenomenal instructor. Later, I approached the instructor and explained my dilemma to her, and she stated that the information I was looking for was often obtained from dance workshops and conferences. She gave me information about an upcoming dance conference in Philadelphia. She stated that registration was closed, but she encouraged me to call anyway.

The next day, I called the number and was surprised by who answered the phone: Pastor Yvette Gaines! I explained to her that I had just received the information about the conference and wanted to see if there was a way that I could still attend. She said that I was more than welcomed to register in person. I then proceeded to tell her about our brief meeting in November of the previous year and how I chickened out when I called her the first time. She responded, "Look at God. He was going to make sure we got connected." Before getting off the phone, she told me to make sure that I introduced myself to her upon my arrival at the conference.

I attended my very first praise dance conference with my Praise Dance class instructor and another student. The

International Dance Conference was hosted by Pastor Yvette Gaines in March of 2005. I had a worship experience like none I've ever had before that launched me into a new level of praise & worship in my personal life. After meeting Pastor Yvette, she and I immediately clicked. On the last night of the conference, her husband made a declaration that God had called her to be a mentor to twelve ladies in dance ministry. When I heard that, I knew I was one of the twelve; as a matter of fact, I dubbed myself as #1, and that was the start of our dance mentor/mentee relationship.

In September of 2005, I attended a dance conference in Atlanta, Dancing Preachers International, hosted by Pastor Sabrina McKenzie. It was there that God gave me the release to join the dance ministry at my local church. He also gave me the assignment to lead an evangelical street dance ministry outside of the church. While attending, a workshop taught by Dr. Ann Higgins, I received a word from her in which she stated that God will put you in the company of others who understand your language of dance. At that time, I had no idea what that meant, but this word resonated in my spirit, and I have held onto it all these years. At the conclusion of a flag ministry workshop I attended, the facilitator, Ann Stevenson, asked us to come up for prayer. When she got to me and began praying, she uttered "God wants to use you like he used Moses to lead others out of bondage." She told me that I will have to be like a pigeon and not look to the right or to the left but keep my eyes focused on God."

These things that were spoken over me at that time were heard and received but not fully acted upon. I had not started the dance ministry that God assigned me to do. I have only been a part of the dance ministry in my church, and I definitely had not become like a pigeon. I'd completely taken my focus off God as I had allowed people, situations, and circumstances to affect me negatively and affect my assignment. Ten plus years have passed, and I haven't fully stepped out on operating in this assignment. But I have been preparing again for it by taking more dance classes and a leadership training program. I've even gotten the name I desire for my dance ministry.

Purpose Principle

I love to dance. In my past, I danced for men. I now have the opportunity to dance for God, and I am thrilled about it. This new realm of dance was very different for me. Going to the dance conferences gave me the exposure I needed to see this new area of dance that God was taking me to; however, I was slightly intimidated by watching the ministry of many seasoned dancers. So, the thought of starting a new dance ministry scared me, especially since there were already thousands of other established and fruitful dance ministries.

When the seed of a Godly idea is birthed in you, you may not give it much thought if it is something that has already been done or if someone else is already doing it. Understand that God can use multiple people who are doing the same things and at the same time to fulfill His will. There will always be a distinctive difference between each ministry. "For My thoughts are not your thoughts, nor are your ways My ways," says the Lord" (Isaiah 55:8). There are many dancers, prophets, pastors, entrepreneurs, singers, actors, chefs, writers, executives, or life coaches doing the same thing at the exact same time, but they all are affecting a totally different group of people; they are doing what they do for those who are divinely assigned to them.

There is a uniqueness to everyone's gift, talent, occupation, brand, business, or ministry, and doing the same thing as someone else will always yield different results. Your purpose is so specific and unique that even if someone else is doing the same thing, the outcome will not be the same. There is a specific group of people assigned to you whose lives you are supposed to impact with your unique purpose. Those people assigned to you will be drawn to your personality and purpose, and they will be impacted by what you are doing. But as it is written: "Eye has not seen, nor ear heard, nor have entered into the heart of man the things which God has prepared for those who love Him" (1 Corinthians 2:9).

When you know your purpose, you will need to have the discipline necessary to walk in it even when you don't feel like it or it doesn't look like anything is happening. You must continue in it. Your purpose journey will be an important key to your success in life. God rewards those who diligently seek Him (Hebrews 11:6), so living a purposeful yet disciplined life will yield great rewards from God. It will feel uncomfortable at first and may even be challenging, but you cannot allow circumstances to dictate how you walk in purpose.

I know that when I stepped out into my purpose, adversity came in various forms. There were times when I could stand, and there came a time where I decided to give up. But after a lot of encouraging words from others, mentoring, and the corralling of the Holy Spirit, I had to remember that my purpose was not about me. My purpose and calling is for God to use my life to impact a group of people who were out there waiting for me — one being you, the reader of this book. So, I had to get out of my feelings, press through, and gird myself up for this new journey. *"And let us not grow weary while doing good, for in due season we shall reap if we do not lose heart"* (Galatians 6:8).

The focus and determination to continue despite distractions, limitations, or adversity will be vitally important. *"Keep thy heart with all diligence; for out of it are the issues of life"* (Proverbs 4:23). Be aware that fear may try to come in, especially in the areas where you may have to step out of your comfort zone, expose yourself, or even be transparent for truth's sake. *"So, we may boldly say: The Lord is my helper; I will not fear. What can man do to me?"* (Hebrews 13:6). Fear cannot be allowed to take root and must be cast aside; you must stand firm to walk with the boldness and assuredness that you are doing exactly what God wants you to be doing at the exact time in which you are doing it. *"…Be strong and of good courage; do not be afraid, nor be dismayed, for the Lord your God is with you wherever you go"* (Joshua 1:9). We know that there is a time and a season for everything under the heaven (Ecclesiastes 3:1) and that includes everyone's individual purpose. The purpose in you was never designed to remain dormant. God wants to awaken the purpose in you so that it may produce the results that God preordained.

ೞ Un-Purposeful ૭

*Esther was an orphan who was raised by her cousin Mordecai who was taken captive from Jerusalem. However, God had a plan for Esther to deliver the Jews from being destroyed. Esther was beautiful, and God **purposed** her beauty to be used to earn her favor in the sight of the King whom she married to reverse the decree written to destroy her people.*
(Esther 2:8-9, 4:14-16, 5:2, 8:5-17)

For years, I saw myself as a failure, but more importantly, as unsuccessful and insignificant. This was due to my lack of a promising career and my doing things that I thought would lead to success based on what I saw in other people's lives, or at least my perception of their lives. I think that I can safely say that at some point in life, everyone has questioned their existence, asking: "Why am I here? Where do I belong? What am I supposed to be doing?" Oftentimes, these questions come when people feel insignificant, they lack success, and they have not experienced fulfillment according to the world's definition of success. For a long time, I asked those same questions. Every day, I would go to work at a job where I saw myself as insignificant; I was in the lowest position of the department, and I didn't make a satisfactory salary. As a woman in her 40s, educated with a college degree, years of work experience, highly skilled, and creative, I lamented thinking this cannot be what God wants me to do for the rest of my life. I want to enjoy life, live my best life, and definitely enjoy what I do for a living. *"So, I saw that there is nothing better for people than to be happy in their work. That is our lot in life. And no one can bring us back to see what happens after we die"* (Ecclesiastes 3:22 NLT).

Many of us look at what we see that others have, and we deem that as success. We only look at their material possessions, and that obscures our thinking about ourselves, our success, or the lack thereof. We don't often look at what people did to get to where they are, how long it took them to get there, or the struggles they may have gone through (if any) along the way. All we see is the end result or the exterior things. *We see the glory but don't know the story.* We have become a society of people who are more in the pursuit of success and money versus the pursuit of true purpose. Happiness and fulfillment has been altered by the world to be based on what you have or what you have accomplished. People are being defined by what they do, what type of job or business they have, what kind of car they drive, what type of house they live in, and what material possessions they've acquired. The devil has people chasing decoys and trying to find their purpose based on status, money, power, fame, or possessions.

God created everyone with a specific and unique purpose; however, purpose has been lost and replaced by the chase for success, notoriety, and acquisition of money and stuff. Purpose is simply defined as what we are created to be and do by He who created us. We are the product of God's creation, and our purpose can only be defined by God. The world's perspective of success and purpose is a misrepresentation of God's designed purpose for our lives.

I listened to many sermons on purpose, but it wasn't until I read the book *Kingdom Woman* that I realized I wasn't doing anything of significance with my life. In reflecting on my life's journey, I began to ask myself, "What is my purpose?" The only thing I knew that I was supposed to do with my life was start an evangelic dance ministry, which God revealed to me in 2005, but I hadn't even done that. Although I had the know-how, I just did not have the drive. Other than that, I felt no value or significance for my life. Growing up, I had many hobbies that included selling candy, styling hair, dancing, and writing. As I got older, I became infatuated with nails, makeup, and graphic design. I am a very creative individual who is artistic in my own way. Out of all the things I developed a keen desire for, I could have chosen a career in any of those areas. I could have been a hair stylist, entrepreneur, professional dancer, writer, nail technician, or graphic artist.

I didn't become a hair stylist because my parents would not support it as they were convinced that working in a hair salon would not be a profitable career. I tried my hand at being an entrepreneur as a nail technician, a graphic artist, and a makeup artist; I even had a bath & body product business. However, I failed at both due to my lack of understanding in business and lack of commitment. In addition, my fears of rejection and low self-esteem caused me to not believe in myself or my business. Although I loved dancing and writing, I just did not give much thought into pursuing either as potential careers. Just like myself, I know there are many people who had aspirations as a kid based on what appealed most to them. "What do you want to be when you grow up?" is a question that every person has been asked as a child. How often do children grow up to be exactly what they said as a kid? Surprisingly, not many of us end up working in the career of our childhood dreams. Surveys have shown that only 30% of people work in the dream job of their childhood because kids go through phases. Many people will have an average of 12 to 15 jobs throughout their lives.

I personally have worked at least 30 jobs. Unfortunately, I spent most of my time working as a temporary worker on a vast number of short-term and long-term contract assignments for staffing agencies for at least 15 years of my life. I have held 12 full-time jobs in my lifetime over 11 combined years of working, with 3 years being my longest tenure on a job. I never believed that I was supposed to be working for someone else, which I have now discovered is true. God had always called me to entrepreneurship; I just hadn't found the correct industry for me. Knowing this, I am now pushing hard to move forward in my purpose.

I now have clarity and understanding of the purpose for my life. There are people who can benefit from my testimony and the story of others. So, I have created my own publishing company as a platform to not only publish my writings but as a platform to help others share their stories with the world as well. As we grow and have new experiences, we think about all the potential careers we can have and all the things we can become. As we grow older and learn new information, along the way, our desires and environments change, and we acquire new interests, skills, and abilities. We may even discover our gifts or a talent. These experiences ultimately shape and affect our career path and who we eventually become. There is also the divine development of our gifts and passions through a spiritual relationship with God to form what we were predestined to do in life.

Over the course of my life, I've been presented with many opportunities to become who I was purposed to be. I didn't heed the opportunities and missed out on what God wanted to do with and through my life. Also, my lack of consistency and commitment to personal endeavors led me to miss many promising opportunities. Now in my early 40s, I've discovered that a lack of purpose can be mentally and emotionally distressful, so it is why I sought God to discover the purpose for my life. I know that every decoy, derailment, mistake, and setback has been used to prepare me for such a time as this, my season of growth, development, fruitfulness, and fulfillment. I am meant to impact the lives of others by sharing my story through gift of writing and ministering.

Just as I've gone through most of my adult life feeling un-purposeful, I'm reassured that I am not alone and that there are others out there who've questioned their existence, their significance, but more importantly, whether they have purpose.

Purpose Principle

I went through many endeavors in my life, and I lacked consistency in developing a successful career. This would appear as though there was no specific purpose for my life, and with all that

*I've done and gone through, I lived my life as if it had no purpose. Our life has purpose, and it is imperative that we have a clear revelation and understanding of that. There are many lives that are being lived day in and day out in just a routine or mundane manner **devoid of purpose.** For me, my purpose was discovered after I was in a place of rebellion and moving away from God. God exposed what I was involved in, and this caused me to be brought to my knees at a place of brokenness (this is discussed in full detail in Chapter 12). It was after that place of turmoil in my life that I came to understand my purpose in life.*

This is not to say that those who are living mundane lives have no purpose, but their purpose is just hanging in the balance because it is unknown to them. Many may not know their purpose for several reasons: they are unsure if they even should have one, they lack understanding, or they fail to seek after God for their purpose. There is purpose for everything created; there is nothing that exists that does not have a unique and specific purpose. We are no different. Everyone has unique gifts, skills, and abilities that are specific to them. It could be the tone of a singer's voice, the technique of a dancer, or the skillfulness of a musician. No two people have the exact same gift, talent, skill or ability. There is a difference and uniqueness in everyone for their specific life's purpose. "Every good gift, every perfect gift, comes from above. These gifts come down from the Father…" (James 1:17).

When we live our life apart from our purpose, if we'd be honest with ourselves, there is some form of unfulfillment to our life and a longing for something more. That longing is God. However, we don't recognize that emptiness we feel inside is God, so we fill our life with various activities, people, careers, sex, drugs, alcohol, money, power, fame, possessions, and food. The void of purpose can only be filled first with receiving the spirit of God then by accomplishing the first purpose for our life and refraining from living apart from God.

God's purpose for our life is to exist for the benefit of others, to show love and to do good unto others. Discovery of purpose requires a readiness to search deep within for what is truly missing from your life. It is God's will to be able to work in you and through you. If you continue to go through life not knowing your purpose, you limit your opportunities to be used by God for the benefit of helping others. That is not how God desires for you to live. It is essential that you seek to identify God's purpose for your life so that He may use you for the greater good of affecting someone else's life for His Glory.

You can discover your purpose through analyzing your talents, skills, and abilities or through righteous indignation. It can even be discovered through what you're passionate about, the qualities others see in you, or your hidden potential that has yet to be uncovered. Experiencing trauma or a tragedy in life can also lead to discovering one's purpose. Your purpose can be revealed through any of these elements in your life or a culmination of multiple elements, and God will use any event from your life to fulfill His purpose and plan.

❧ The Divine Interruption ❧

Create in me a pure heart, O God, and renew a steadfast spirit within me. Do not cast me from your presence or take your Holy Spirit from me. Restore to me the joy of your salvation and grant me a willing spirit, to sustain me. Then I will teach transgressors your ways, so that sinners will turn back to you. (Psalm 51:10-13)

Every life has a purpose. Letting go of past mistakes, failures, hurts, and offenses is vital to purpose. Oftentimes, we allow our past to paralyze us from effectively going forward into our future. There comes a time when you must leave everything from the past behind you and focus on what's ahead for you. There is a purposeful future for your life, so you cannot spend time worrying about what mistakes you made, what wrongs were done to you, or the things you didn't do. Embrace what you now have the ability to do. Embrace the spirit of truth, embrace grace, and allow your life to be transformed with purposeful intent. *"Don't copy the behavior and customs of this world, but let God transform you into a new person by changing the way you think. Then you will learn to know God's will for you, which is good and pleasing and perfect."* (Romans 12:2 MSG).

Going to church doesn't make us saved; it's our relationship, righteousness, and holiness unto God that does so. It had been more than 18 years since I stopped dancing and completely dedicated my life to Christ. In the beginning and for many years, I was on fire for God. As the years went on, I learned there were still some areas of my life I had not surrendered to God. I recognized that I could not live in the freedom of Jesus Christ because I hadn't dealt with strongholds, and I was not delivered from the spirits that oppressed me. Thus, I still had negative and unrighteous behavior patterns that manifested from deep-rooted triggers: feelings of rejection, abandonment, and low self-esteem.

Many years later, I allowed various events in my life to impair my relationship with God. I was broken by negative circumstances occurring at home, work, and church. My marriage had broken down because of issues my husband and I refused to handle as they arose. We moved past things as if they never happened, and we never faced our problems. The saying "hurt people, hurt people" rang true in my marriage. It became a continuous cycle of my husband and I hurting one another verbally, mentally, emotionally, and sometimes physically until we came to a point where the marriage was near destruction. I unintentionally, but coincidently, became the cause of that destruction. Normal communication did not exist in our household; a simple question such as "Where are you?" or "When is this bill going to get paid" would almost always end in an argument if either of us wasn't satisfied with the response that was given. During this period, I had mentally, physically, and emotionally divorced myself from my husband. The only thing left to do was to leave and file the papers.

My husband worked a lot, a whole lot; he spent more time working than he did at home. He did so to provide for his family and give me the best of everything: luxury home, luxury car, and name brand handbags, shoes, and clothes. However, all those things were unable to fill the void of not having his presence fully in the home, which triggered lingering seeds of rejection and abandonment. This was coupled with the fact that my primary love language was quality time, and I wasn't receiving any from my husband. His excessive working gave me thoughts that he no longer wanted to be around me, and this weighed heavily on my esteem. I did not recognize or realize this was a two-fold setup. It was a setup to either seek God to fill the attention void or seek the attention from others. Unfortunately, I chose the latter. I allowed my emotions to make the choice for me, and I sought out the attention of someone other than my spouse "because I needed someone to talk to." I met someone who would fill the void of attention and give me the quality time I was not getting at home.

When we find ourselves faced with certain situations, we have a few choices to make: the choice of life or death, the choice of good or evil, and the choice of right or wrong. Oftentimes, we allow our emotions and flesh to dictate our feelings, and we make decisions that could have adverse effects on our life. Regardless of the decisions we make or have made, repentance and forgiveness are available to us all through God's love and grace, and God makes all things well again.

Aside from my marriage, I was also very unhappy on my job; I was working a job where I had way too many skills and experience for the position and not enough pay. I felt like getting this job was a punishment from God. At the time, I got the job, I was engaged in inappropriate indiscretions with my Pastor at that time. He and I worked closely together alone at the church office for almost two years. I felt like God put me on this job to get me away from the Pastor so that I wouldn't be the cause of his fall. Prior to getting this job, which I told God I didn't want it after the interview, I applied for so many other jobs. I had the qualifications, skills, and experience for the open positions I applied for, but I never received any calls from my application or after the interview. The reason I took the job I didn't want when it was offered to me was because I was receiving unemployment benefits at the time. One of the stipulations of unemployment is that you cannot turn down a job offer for any reason. I literally despised this job, but regardless of how I saw it, there came a point where it was actually a blessing in disguise. When I needed to leave my home temporarily, my manager allowed me to work remotely for an extended period.

I have also experienced many offenses in ministry, and several of these offenses at varying periods crushed my spirit sorely. The first offense I experienced happened when God released me to join the dance ministry in my church. The leader and I bumped heads, so before I could dance my first dance, I was kicked out, or sat down in church lingo, and I remained so for 3 years. When I was allowed back in the dance ministry, I did well until a personal conflict with the leader caused me to be sat down again for another period of a year. When I was finally able to return, I remained under her leadership for a short period until she eventually vacated the position.

In my mind, I was hoping that I would be chosen as the new leader, but that did not happen; another dance member was selected. I served well under the new leader, and she was very open and flexible in allowing me to choreograph a great number of the dances we ministered. I had also been faithful and submitted to her leadership. Then, the new leader had to vacate the position for personal reasons. A new leader was not immediately appointed, so I stepped up to carry out the responsibilities in leading the team.

Then, another smack in the face came; I was passed over for the dance leader position once again when another member of the dance ministry was appointed as the new leader. After this incident, other duties and responsibilities began to be taken from me without explanation. I wondered and even questioned when does faithfulness and commitment account for something in the ministry. I was a very faithful and committed member in my attendance, giving, and serving. I was also faithful and loyal in serving my Pastor to the point where it caused us to have an inappropriate relationship. I thought at least my relationship with him would put me in that leadership position. It didn't. Feelings of rejection began to show again. I felt like I wasn't good enough for the ministry, I felt used, and I no longer felt like I had a place there. These incidents caused anger, hurt, and bitterness to settle within me, and I became spiritually dysfunctional and disconnected from the ministry.

I allowed the hurt from my marriage, my work, and the church offenses to take my focus off God. The hurt turned to anger, and before long, bitterness finally settled in.

I was bitter towards my husband at home. I was bitter at work because I didn't like the job. I was bitter at church towards my Pastor, his wife, the new dance ministry leader, and pretty much everyone else in the ministry. But you would never have known it because I put on my "church mask." I masked my true feelings all the while committing spiritual suicide. I went through the motions as if everything was ok. I went to church and never missed a service or event. I was going through the motions of praying, praise & worship, dance, and listening to the preached word, but my heart wasn't there. My intimate fellowship with God was distant. I still communed with God, but it was just out of habitual behavior because that is what I had been doing for years. Everything I gave to God at that point was empty and devoid of substance.

I became broken by these "wrongdoings" against me. I erected a wall around my heart and refused to even allow God to penetrate through it. I would not allow myself to be hurt again from situations that occurred in my life, especially in the church. I now understand that the things that I was going through were designed to help me grow and develop spiritually, but I looked at them as "they did me wrong." I was mad at God! Never did I take it as an opportunity to grow and develop in God. I should have known that God would use these situations to build and develop me for the greater good of His will and purpose for my life. Instead of looking at the times of adversity as an opportunity for growth, I acted out. I wasn't hurting God; I was only hurting myself and others in the process. I couldn't even be honest with myself; I was my own blessing blocker.

I thought more of myself, control, and a position than I did of my relationship with God and my family. I had already run away spiritually, mentally, and emotionally, and running away physically was the next step. I rebelled and acted out until my life had spun out of control. God will not go against a person's will. God will allow us to do whatever it is that we want to do. However, God will also make sure that His plan and will is fulfilled in the earth. When God reveals your purpose, regardless of where you are or what you are doing, God will interrupt your life when His Kairos (time) for His purpose in your life is due. That is exactly what He did with me. Since I was created to make a difference and there is a unique potential in me that only I can fulfill, I believe that God loved me so much He was not going to allow me to get away easily. He had a call for my life, a purpose, vision, and assignment that He wants fulfilled through me.

I had come to a place of complete brokenness. God said "Okay daughter, you are exactly where I need you." In my brokenness, I had a heartfelt encounter with God and came to a place of total repentance. I poured my whole heart out to God, and He covered me with His love. As a result, God orchestrated a plan of restoration for my relationship with Him. In August of 2015, my family and I made the decision for me to go away for a personal revival with God. I traveled back to my hometown in Houston for six weeks of deliverance, healing, cleansing, and impartation of the Holy Spirit.

The process included the elimination of all distractions: people, television, internet, social media, and anything that would take my focus off God. I spent this time saturating myself with the word, listening to the word, studying the word, praying and worshipping. I only left my place of refuge to attend services for spiritual building; I attended services on Wednesday, Friday, Saturday and Sunday, and any additional special services the Lord led me to go to. I kept myself at a place of intense focus on rebuilding my relationship with God. I also limited my visits from family and friends. At the end of my process of restoration, I was delivered, healed, made whole, and liberated. My marriage was restored also, and my husband flew to Houston to "get his wife back." While we were there, we renewed our wedding vows on September 26, 2015 at a Vow Renewal Service at New Light Christian Center.

I was healed from hurt, and my heart was cleaned of all bitterness, resentment, and anger. I have a renewed relationship with God, and I love God with all my heart. My relationship with my husband and daughter was restored as well. I now live a healthy and whole relationship with God. I thought that I would have this relationship automatically after I got saved over 18 years ago, but that wasn't the case. My healthy and whole relationship with God is the result of surrendering those "untouchable" areas of my life and revealing the desires of my flesh. Months later, I received the revelation of God's divine interruption in my life. In 2016, my family experienced a tremendous amount of adversity and tribulation. Had I been in my old mindset with a strained relationship with God, I would have crumbled and been destroyed. However, when this adversity hit, I was in a great place in my relationship with God with a powerful and active prayer & praise life. Although it as a painful process, I thank God for His *divine interruption* in my life.

Purpose Principle

God cannot heal you from indiscretions that you have not revealed to Him. You must admit your weaknesses and sins to God and ask for help. God will send you help, and you must submit to the process of deliverance by surrendering your personal will. There is a renewing of the mind when you surrender your will to God's. Renewing your mind is not a one-time event; it is an ongoing process that continues throughout life. We should always be in the constant pursuit of renewing our mind. Just like 1 Thessalonians 5:17 tells us to pray without ceasing, we should never cease to renew our minds from negativity, bad habits and behaviors, old ways of thinking, and self-fulfilling thoughts and actions. We need to get to a point where we yield our bodies, thoughts, and actions to God.

God wants everyone to live a life of complete wholeness and liberation in Him. The number one thing that I am most grateful for in my life is my restored relationship with God. If you have gotten to of a place where your relationship with God is strained or broken, you must desire to open your heart back up to Him. God will give you a process for restoration. You must first admit your faults and come to a place of genuine repentance where you are willing to turn away from anything and anyone that would hinder your focus and relationship with God.

☙ My Purpose ❧

*Who has saved us, and called us with a holy calling, not according to our works, but according to his own **purpose** and grace, which was given to us in Christ Jesus before the world began.*
(2 Timothy 1:9)

One night in December 2015, I had a vision of me standing before a group of women telling my story. The next morning, the Lord spoke to me and said to write a book about *the pathway to purpose*, and it will be about discovering your gift and purpose, protecting it, and knowing your worth and value in God. I nonchalantly made notes in my journal and didn't give it any further thought. The same day, the Lord compelled me to take out my journal and write, which I did, and I wrote out many of the details of my journey told in this book.

In writing this book, I had a conversation with my husband about purpose. I said to him, "What if I never traveled the road that I'd taken in dancing? Was dance really my purpose?" He responded by saying that although I had gone down a wrong path in my life by not knowing any better, God would use my testimony to help others so that He gets the glory from it. *"But as for you, you meant evil against me; but God meant it for good, in order to bring it about as it is this day, to save many people alive"* (Genesis 50:20). While I accepted his response, I was still unsettled about my purpose. I couldn't see how my self-proclaimed purpose to be a dancer could be what God had planned for my life. Now I understand that God will use your natural gifts, even the ones that you misused out of ignorance, in the kingdom for His glory. Even though I knew that God has used me to dance and had given me a dance ministry assignment, I still wondered: *What if I never discovered that I could dance at an early age? What if I rejected dance? What if I never embarked on the journey I traveled? What if I had never followed through with that second dance audition with the Sexxx Fiends? What was my original purpose from birth?*

The next morning after the conversation with my husband, I was lounging in bed, meditating, studying, and writing excerpts for the book when I said to God, "I still would like to know what my original purpose was." His response was, "You're doing it." God spoke to my heart and said that writing was my original purpose. I was then reminded of my childhood and teen years where I'd written poetry, essays, and stories, and when I was recognized through published works and contest winnings for my writings. I also remembered my daddy telling me as a teenager that I was going to be a journalist or a writer. I have now reunited with my purpose and everything has been made clear.

God is so amazing in that He has merged the chain of events of my life to bring me back full circle to the purpose he preordained for me: to be a writer. My purpose in writing is to inspire, impart, and impact the lives of others who will read my published works on how to live a purposeful life. My calling and assignment is to decree and declare the word of God and evangelize to the lost. My purpose as a writer is to impact and inspire others through my writings as a scribe and an oracle of God. This book is not only the product of my testimony, but it is the fulfillment of me stepping into my purpose. I have now discovered my purpose, and I can't be happier. I now have revelation of Jeremiah 1:5 as it pertains to my life.

God was apparently pulling me towards my pathway to purpose years ago, but I didn't recognize it. I had started writing fiction novels, and in the one story, the characters discover their purpose in God. I knew that these novels were something that God wanted me to write, but I never completed them due to procrastination, a lack of drive, and adversity. Although I enjoyed writing, at that moment, I didn't feel fulfilled in it. My purpose had been beckoning me even when I didn't recognize it. I started the first novel in 2006 and would write on it from time to time. I also started a second novel in 2012. In 2009, I spent a lot of time on my first novel and had done a large amount of writing. One day, I was abruptly dismissed from a temp job I was working at the time, and out of anger, I did something that caused me to lose a great deal of content for that book. Instead of preserving my files from my work computer, I deleted them all, and I didn't have a backup of the most updated version of the book. I let years pass before I started writing on the novel again, but I had lost the motivation and decided writing wasn't for me. Even after promptings by the Holy Spirit, I still procrastinated in doing so.

At one point in life, I became comfortable in thinking that I had no significant purpose in life. Even though I served in ministry for many years, I still felt I lacked purpose; I often felt I lacked significance even in the church. This thought was totally from the enemy who was trying to keep me from discovering the purpose of God for my life and fulfilling the assignment He'd given me to keep me in a place of bondage through complacency. Being in a state of complacency can stifle your purpose. It stops you from pursuing your purpose by stealing your motivation and passion for your purpose. Complacency can fool you into thinking that life will always be this way and that there is no point in trying to do anything further, different, or better. When complacency settles in, you get to a point of wanting to give up and sometimes even quit life, which is where demonic thoughts of suicide enter in. I even entertained those thoughts on several occasions.

In an effort to find some meaning in my life, I focused on fulfilling a new passion and finding my contentment in it. Makeup had become my passion; I now desired to become a successful makeup artist. I set out to do all that I could to turn my *passion into profits*. I was going this route because it was the mantra advertised by many successful people I looked up to in the business and entrepreneurial world. My focus switched to being successful in the world, and the world's view of success is to prosper and profit from doing something "you're passionate about." Yet, I struggled to succeed in this area. I think God prevented me from taking a path that I was trying to carve out for myself, once again, and it was tremendously frustrating. I knew what God had "called" me to do, but I was fighting against where God was trying to lead me. Being called into ministry is not as exciting at first, especially when it's taking you in a direction you don't want to go in. God was setting me on the path for it anyway. I lost the fight, and God won; I've yielded to God by allowing Him to change the direction of my life from what I wanted to do to what He wants me to do. I've conceded my will for His.

The good news is that started back working on the novels I started writing, I was able to recall the lost content, and I am thriving while writing those novels. I have also been journaling content for new novels, blog posts, content writing, and courses that God has spoken to me about writing. I even wrote and independently published a fiction book in 2016 that is doing well and blessing all those who read it.

Purpose Principle

God wants you to walk in your purpose and fulfill His will for your life, but God will not force you to walk the path He has set you on. We are free mortal beings who have a choice of whether we follow God or not. God will not go against a person's will. The loving nature of God will implore you to yield to Him, release your own will, and submit to His will for your life. "Now may the God of peace...make you complete in every good work to do His will, working in you what is well pleasing in His sight, through Jesus Christ, to whom be glory forever and ever. Amen" (Hebrews 13:20-21).

The book of Jeremiah shows us that purpose is given before we are born. "Before I formed you in the womb I knew you; Before you were born I sanctified you; I ordained you a prophet to the nations" (Jeremiah 1:5). You were on God's mind long before He was on your mind. Every person is born with a purpose that was bestowed upon you before you were formed in your mother's womb. You were not created merely from the coming together of your mother and father but for a God ordained purpose. God created every being for His glory and to expand the Kingdom of God here on the earth. God pre-designed our pathway of life. To those who believe in Him, it is His desire that we walk this path by faith. To those who have yet to believe in Him, this is a call that you do so from this moment forward. First and foremost, we must choose to live our life in God. "I call heaven and earth to record this day against you, that I have set before you life and death, blessing and cursing: therefore, choose life that both you and you seed may live" (Deuteronomy 30:19).

☙ The Assignment ❧

But rise and stand on your feet; for I have appeared to you for this purpose, to make you a minister and a witness both of the things which you have seen and of the things which I will yet reveal to you. I will deliver you from the Jewish people, as well as from the Gentiles, to whom I now send you, to open their eyes, in order to turn them from darkness to light, and from the power of Satan to God, that they may receive forgiveness of sins and an inheritance among those who are sanctified by faith in Me.
(Acts 26:16-19)

When we experience failures in our life, there is always an opportunity to start anew. We must recognize when God gives us that opportunity to start again with a clean slate and to run the race that He has set before us. The purpose for our lives was established before we were ever born. It is how we navigate through life that determines how and when we reach our destiny. God's purpose, will, and calling for our lives is unchangeable, regardless of how we perform. *"For God's gift and his call are irrevocable"* (Romans 11:29 NIV). Since we are the righteousness of God, we should behave accordingly.

While I was away in Houston in 2015, one thing God spoke to me was that He still expected me to fulfill the dance ministry assignment he had given me in 2005. This overwhelmed me as I was amazed that after all these years, all I had been through, and especially all I had done, God still wanted to use me to carry out that part of His will and plan for my life. When your heart is clean and right before God, you will begin to grow spiritually in every area of your life as you position yourself to be used by God for His glory. I learned that our failures, mistakes, or shortcomings do not cancel out God's plan and assignment for us; we just need to give God the control over getting our lives in order so that we can carry out the assignment.

The bible states that the body is for the Lord. "...*The body, however, is not meant for sexual immorality but for the Lord, and the Lord for the body,*" (1 Corinthians 6:13 NIV). The gifts from heaven are for the glory of God and not just for our own pleasure or enjoyment. "*Every good gift, every perfect gift, comes from above. These gifts come down from the Father*" (James 1:17 CEB). In the world today, there is a perversion of the body and the gifts of God, especially amongst women as it pertains to dance. The body and gift of dance has deceptively been perverted as a means to make money as it brings delight to others. This was not the original plan of God for the precious body of a woman or His unique gift of dance. Dance was designed to show praises unto God (Psalms 149:3, 150:4), to celebrate victories (Exodus 15:19-21), and to honor God with worship (2 Samuel 6:12-16).

People feel they have the right to do what they want with their bodies without accountability or the knowledge that there will be consequences for their lifestyle choices. "*There is a way that seems right to a man, but its end is the way of death*" (Proverbs 14:12 NKJV). It is not God's will that anyone continue in this mindset or way of life. God has now given me the clarion call to appeal to ladies dancing in strip clubs as well as ladies who don't recognize and understand their value and worth. I know through my own personal experience that those who pursue these lifestyles do so because of low self-esteem, rejection, trauma and abandonment issues.

God showed me that these ladies in these clubs were just as important to Him as I was, and just like He used someone's life to lead me out, He wants to use my life to lead these ladies out as well. God frees people from their bondages for himself. I was in bondage to issues of rejection, self-esteem, abandonment, and the need for attention. God used someone's life to free me from the bondage of that lifestyle before it took me to a place much further than I already was. I was living the high-life with money and popularity, but although I didn't recognize it at the time, I was living in darkness. *"And you, my child, will be called a prophet of the Most High; for you will go on before the Lord to prepare the way for him, to give his people the knowledge of salvation through the forgiveness of their sins, because of the tender mercy of our God, by which the rising sun will come to us from heaven to shine on those living in darkness and in the shadow of death, to guide our feet into the path of peace"* (Luke 1:76-79 NIV).

There are many whose lives are in the same darkness I was in, and there are others who are living in even darker places in their lives. God delivered me out of darkness for a purpose; His purpose. I believe that my life and voice are a light that will shine upon people that live in the darkness of their minds. There are many who believe that God blesses them regardless of their unrighteousness and despite their actions. There is error in the way people live, think, and act, and correction must be revealed so that repentance can take place.

The clarion call God has given me brought clarity for me regarding the word received from Dr. Ann in 2005: "God will put you in the company of others who understand your language of dance, and God wants to use you like He used Moses to lead others out of bondage." At first, when God spoke this to me, it felt like such a burden, and one I didn't think I could handle. However, God reminded me of what He's placed inside of me, His spirit. I discovered the scripture in Romans 11:2 and 5, which states, "*God will not cast away his people which he foreknew, even so then at this present time also there is a remnant according to the election of grace.*" This didn't lessen the burden that I felt for the assignment, but I have since embraced this assignment and made it a desire of my heart because it is God's desire. I then had my yielding moment just as Jesus had on the Mount of Olives when he prayed "*Father, if you are willing, take this cup from me: yet not my will, but yours be done" (Luke 22:42).* Although I have rediscovered my purpose in God, I've come to realize that my calling and assignment from God are greater because souls depend on it. I desire to see others free from the issues of their past or their current situations so that they may live fruitful lives.

1 Corinthians 1:27 tells us that "*God uses the foolish things of the world.*" I definitely did not see myself as worthy of this assignment or the clarion call, but I believe that God has qualified me for this assignment because He gave it to me. I was not perfect, I absolutely didn't do everything right,

and I made many bad decisions; however, I did make good decisions as well. When I was dancing, although I was a part of that toxic environment, I did not allow myself to become a product of the environment. I did not drink or use drugs, even though seeds of drinking and drug use were sown into me early in life from what I witnessed from my father and family members. I did not engage in prostitution, pornography, or same sex relationships; these seeds were sown into me at a very young age, but apparently, there was a strong will in me to not involve myself as a participant in any of those activities.

Before a dancer would perform a table dance, she would sit and talk to the customer. On many occasions, I would have customers say to me, "You are such an intelligent girl," and ask why I was in that environment. My response would be simple: "I love to dance so why not get paid to do it." Besides, I worked in corporate America by day and was taking college classes, so I didn't see myself as the same as many of the other girls. There were quite a few of the ladies I danced with who were like me; there were those who were just in it for the money and would not allow themselves to become totally engulfed in the lifestyle. The relationship I was in at the time and being a mother also helped to keep me grounded.

Growing up, I didn't have many friends, and I wasn't easily accepted. I realize now that I used the dance platform to get the attention that I thought I needed in my life. I didn't get much attention from the people that I thought I should, so I created a platform that I thought would bring me all the attention I desired. Although the attention at the time seemed positive because the spotlight was on me, it was negative attention and a channel for other negative things to later come into my life. The attention I received in the beginning days of dancing overwhelmed me so much that I craved it, and thus, I went deeper than I was supposed to go: from dancing in music videos to dancing in the nude. I recognize now that the only attention I needed was from God, and He was trying to get my attention all along the way through every rejection. Yet I chose another way for myself by getting the attention and acceptance that I longed for from people.

I now understand that I wasn't widely accepted and was kept from certain things, places, and people because I was always supposed to be separate and set apart as a part of God's purpose and plan for my life. Although it may be difficult to understand, especially for a young child, you must embrace it when you have been set apart, made different, or not easily accepted by others. It is God's doing; He is separating you from anyone and anything that would pose a threat to the purpose and call for your life. *"But I know that the Lord hath set apart him that is godly for himself"* *(Psalm 4:3)*. God has also given you the responsibility to separate yourself from those things and people that would hinder the call of God and the purpose of God for your life. *"Wherefore come out from among them, and be ye separate, says the Lord"* *(2 Corinthians 6:17)*.

I realize that God has purposed me to use writing and my testimony of dance to fulfill His plan for my life. The perversion of God's gift upon my life has now been turned for good. *"And we know that all things work together for good to*

111

them that love God, to them who are the called according to his purpose" (Romans 8:28). God will use the gift of dance to relay a message of hope to others through interpretive dance movements that will encourage and inspire others and to cause a change of atmosphere in the lives of those who witness it. Souls are important to God because they were created for a purpose.

Just as God corralled me back to my original purpose and calling, He wants to do the same for those ladies and many others who have allowed themselves to be devalued so that they may embrace their value and worth in Him. God wants to do the same for anyone who is not walking in the purpose or calling in which He designed for their life. There must be a yielding moment to get to the place where God wants you. No matter where you are now or where you have been, all is not lost for those who have gotten off the path that leads to God and His will and purpose for their life.

Even after we are saved and have accepted our purpose from God, we may inadvertently allow people or situations to come into our lives and lead us down a different path *(2 Samuel 11:2-5, 12:9, Psalms 51).* I even allowed myself to get off the path to my destiny after receiving God's salvation. It devastated me to know that I allowed ten years to pass while I was off God's path. However, I could no longer dwell on the past, so I moved forward as I was **compelled** to do because of God's love, grace, and mercy.

I've also learned that my journey to purpose was about the prophetic call on my life. God called and ordained me as a Prophetess. I now understand two things: 1. due to this calling, the attack on my life started at an early age and followed me through much of my life, and 2. God restored me by His grace to fulfill His purpose so that I could confidently walk in this calling and anointing on my life. When I first heard this, I did not readily accept it. God sent His word to me by two people, and I rejected it both times. God even spoke it to me directly through scripture. I eventually surrendered, but I was full of doubt. God sent me a final confirmation on October 8, 2016 by way of a prophetic word spoken to me by Dr. Alexis Maston. She spoke about the calling and anointing on my life as a Prophetess, and it has been spoken and recognized by many others since. I've now accepted that this is who God has called me to be, and I must be obedient to Him. *"For You formed my inward parts; You covered me in my mother's womb. I will praise You, for I am fearfully and wonderfully made; Marvelous are Your works, and that my soul knows very well. My frame was not hidden from You, When I was made in secret, and skillfully wrought in the lowest parts of the earth. Your eyes saw my substance, being yet unformed. And in Your book they all were written, the days fashioned for me, when as yet there were none of them"* (Psalms 139:13-16).

Purpose Principle

You are not meant to be bound by your past or any mistakes you made along the way. God wants you to move forward. He is the God of grace, and His will is that you be perfect in Him. It is His intent that you walk in His love and grace to fulfill His will for your life through purpose. "God is my strength and power, and He makes my way perfect." (2 Samuel 22:33).

You will live the best days of your life when you understand that your life is not your own; you belong to God. God wants you to lean on and rely on Him in every area of your life. Your life is a gift from God, but your gift of life is for the purpose of being used by God. God wants to use you and your life to help others and to show forth His mercy. You cannot allow yourself to wallow in pity over past failures or mistakes or feel like you have no purpose and that your life is meaningless. Your life is full of meaning; it is meant to love God, be loved by God, love others, and allow God to love others through you.

⍟ Cultivating Purpose ⍟

"Many are the plans in a person's heart, but it is the LORD's purpose that prevails." (Proverbs 19:21)

The cultivation of purpose should start when we are kids by our parents, but unfortunately, that doesn't always happen, especially for those of us with parents who were not walking in their purpose. I encourage parents to be conscious of who is around your children, both family and non-family, what is spoken into them, and the things they experience. We must be mindful of the seeds that are sown into our children so that they don't produce a harvest that was not intended for their life. Take note of what is being passed down to your children.

When I was pregnant with my second daughter, I exercised to control my weight, and I often danced up until my delivery. I discovered early in my daughter's life that my gift and talent of dance was passed down to her. As she grew older, I cultivated this gift for God's glory by putting her in dance classes, and she danced in church. I had to protect what could be the legacy call of dance on her life. Another thing that I discovered about her is that she too had a gift of writing. Just like me, at a very young age, she started writing stories, but she was more passionate about writing gospel music. Not only is my daughter's dance talent better than mine, but her writing abilities are even greater.

While writing this book, God revealed to me that writing and music are her purpose, and she too has a prophetic call on her life. Just like me, she had stopped writing stories and music, but I was led by God to tell her to continue writing, to encourage her, and cultivate her so that she will always seek to pursue her God-ordained purpose above all and walk in the fulfillment of it. Many people have said that I am overprotective of my daughter. As a spirit-led mother, I have an awareness of familiar spirits, and it is my responsibility to protect her from those lingering spirits by making sure that every potential door of opportunity for encroachment upon her is closed. I know what I was exposed to at an early age, and because of that exposure, my life went in a different direction than it should have. I do not want the same for my daughter, nor do I want any other person's child to experience such a heart-aching journey in life.

The job of the enemy is to deceive us into thinking that we don't have a real purpose; that with all the people on the earth, there isn't a specific reason for our existence. The greatest deception that a person can endure is from thinking that they have no purpose. This type of thinking can lead a person, especially a Christian believer, into carnal living and complacency. *"For those who live according to the flesh set their minds on the things of the flesh, but those who live according to the Spirit, the things of the Spirit. For to be carnally minded is death, but to be spiritually minded is life and peace. Because the carnal mind is enmity against God; for it is not subject to the law of God, nor indeed can be. So then, those who are in the flesh cannot please God"* (Romans 8:5-8).

Carnal living is designed to move you away from God, and this is the agenda of the enemy to prevent you from being an effective witness for Christ, thus, moving you out of your place of purpose. You have purpose in you; carnality and complacency are enemies to purpose and must be ejected from your life. Carnality is designed to exploit the gifts, talents, and abilities in you so that you do not use them for God's glory but to be misused in the world. The job of the enemy is to deceive you into thinking that your talents would yield greater benefits and rewards if they are utilized in the world. This is a lie that has brought about a misconception that the use of your talent for God's glory yields a lesser reward. We see this too often with many of our singers in the world. Many of them have said they started off singing in the church, but end up singing secular music.

Complacency is designed to stifle you so that you do not use your abilities in the manner for which it was designed: for God's glory and Kingdom. *"But to each one of us grace was given according to the measure of Christ's gift. Therefore, He says: 'When He ascended on high, He led captivity captive, and gave gifts to men'"* (Ephesians 4:7-8). If you have identified your gifts, you cannot sit on them; they can no longer remain dormant. It is crucial for you to develop your gifts and promote them for God's glory. Effective workings and use of the gifts, talents, and skills that you possess will require a lifestyle that is fully committed to God by living a life that is blameless, sanctified, and holy unto Him. God is calling, equipping, and preparing you for His purpose. *"Therefore, brethren, be even more diligent to make your call and election sure, for if you do these things you will never stumble"* (2 Peter 1:10).

Giving yourself fully to the usefulness of God is to let go of the past and make peace within so that it will no longer affect your present or your future. Also, you cannot concern yourself with what others think of you; only what God thinks of you matters, and you should seek to please God and Him only. If you are hurting in any area of your life, you must release that to God and allow Him to heal you. You cannot be an effective witness of God if you're still holding onto past hurts; release and forgive. The purpose that God has for your life is about Him using you. You cannot compare yourself to others or be concerned about what's going on in someone else's life. Everyone has their own unique purpose and a journey that leads to that purpose. You cannot form an opinion about them because you have no idea what a person's journey is about or what God is doing in them.

When God gives you instructions, it is in your best interest to yield and obey. When you allow reasoning to take place, you're likely to second-guess the instructions because you may not have all the answers. The mind is not designed to figure out the things of God. You must trust God with your spirit and not your mind; allow the spirit of God to align your thoughts. God has the answers, and He will give them to you just when you need them and sometimes when you least expect. God knows exactly what He wants to do and how He wants it done. When the time comes, He will put the right people and resources in place to fulfill His purpose. It is your posture in God that shows Him that you are willing and able to be used for His glory.

ᥰ Discovering Your Purpose ᥱ

"But seek first the kingdom of God and His righteousness..."
(Matthew 6:33)

Your purpose and destiny were preordained and designed by God, and once you start moving in that direction, there is nothing that can stop it; no mistakes, failures or even people can stop what God has ordained for you. When your heart is right towards God and you are living in His will, it is inevitable for you to fulfill your life's purpose. You find your purpose by allowing God to lead you to it. People often go through things in life, and as hard as it can be to understand why we go through some situations, you must know that God has a purpose for you and those things in which you cannot understand. *"And He said to me," 'My grace is sufficient for you, for My strength is made perfect in weakness..." (2 Corinthians 12:9).* That issue that you are going through is only temporary, but the plans and purposes of God are eternal and everlasting." *And we know that all things work together for good to those who are called according to His purpose"* (Romans 8:28 NKJV).

Have you tried to find or identify your purpose? If so, in what ways have you done so? Contrary to what you may believe, discovering your purpose is relatively easy and is the most important thing you will do in life if you have a complete and intimate relationship with God. On the other hand, if you don't have a relationship with the Lord,

120

discovering your purpose will be a challenge. First and foremost, you must make sure of your salvation and that Jesus Christ is Savior and Lord of your life. For others, discovering their purpose may be a challenge because they allow their inability to let go of things from the past to hinder their journey towards finding their purpose.

Ponder these questions:

- What natural talent or ability do you have?
- What are you good at?
- Is there something that you really enjoy doing?
- Is there something that burdens you and do you want to do something about it?
- Did you go through a situation that you overcame and do you want to help others now?

Your purpose possibly lies within the answer you gave to any of these questions. After you have answered these questions, you are now at a place where you can discover your purpose as God leads you to it. Purpose is produced by faith, so believe God for what it is that you are supposed to be doing.

When reach the point where you want to know your purpose, you need to get to a place of quietness in your mind, heart, and spirit. Get in a quiet place where you can tune out all distractions so that you can clearly hear from God. Once you are clear and quiet within, your purpose will be readily revealed. Seek God in prayer, and He will give you an inner peace that will release understanding and clarity of your purpose. *"Don't worry about anything; instead, pray about everything. Tell God what you need, and thank him for all he has done. Then you will experience God's peace, which exceeds anything we can understand. His peace will guard your hearts and minds as you live in Christ Jesus"* (Philippians 4:6-7).

One of the most important things to do is clear yourself of any negativity that is rooted in you about yourself. *"For as he thinks in his heart, so is he"* (Proverbs 23:7). How you see yourself will affect your effectiveness in walking in your purpose. Having a positive self-image will propel you to impact someone else's life with your purpose because we exist for the benefit of others. People get the overflow of the fruit of your positive self-image and passion for fulfilling your purpose.

Once we make the ultimate choice in life to follow purpose, we must choose and aspire to walk the path that God has placed us on and stay focused on God, His purpose, and His promises. *"Let your eyes look straight ahead; fix your gaze directly before you. Give careful thought to the paths for your feet and be steadfast in all your ways. Do not turn to the right or the left..."* (Proverbs 4: 25-26). Oftentimes, we do not know what the path holds; in fact, we have no idea what our journey will bring or where it will lead us. This path is one with a direction and an end in which we cannot see; however, we must trust God's leading because Psalms 16:11 assures us of this: *"You will show me the path of life."* The journey ahead can seem blurry to us because we don't know where it will lead us, but we must have a strong resolve to stay on the road. Ultimately, we will discover that our journey will lead us to our rightful place in Jesus where we will reach our destiny.

We must remain faithful and consistent in our determination to reach our purposed destiny. God has given us natural and spiritual gifts, passions, and desires to fulfill His purpose, and there are groups of people whom we should be influencing for God's glory. These people are called the harvest, and the reason we have purpose is for the benefit of the harvest. *"But when He saw the multitudes, He was moved with compassion for them, because they were weary and scattered, like sheep having no shepherd. Then He said to His disciples, the harvest truly is plentiful, but the laborers are few. Therefore, pray the Lord of the harvest to send out laborers into his harvest"* (Matthew 9:36-38). We must be serious about our purpose because it is vitally important for us to lead those who are lost to a better life by the impact of us walking in our purpose.

When you are pursuing your purpose, passion, or anything that God has led you to do, you will face both natural and spiritual obstacles, but you must trust that God knows what He is doing when He is allowing you to go through those obstacles. God is building and developing you for the greater good of His will and purpose for your life. Rest in the peace and assurance that God has your best interests in mind, and be keen to obey God in everything. When you take the bold action to step out in faith and walk in your purpose and in obedience to what God has instructed you to do, challenges, adversities, and tribulations will come to pressure or deter you from doing what you need to do. Brace yourself for the faith fight. Stand and be strong in the Lord and the Word of God, and you will endure until the end. "… *'Not by might nor by power, but by My Spirit,' Says the Lord of Hosts"* (Zechariah 4:6).

Prayer is going to have to be an essential element to fulfilling your purpose. Prayer is where you communicate with God. You will not be able to successfully pursue or walk in purpose without having a consistent and strong prayer life. In prayer, you share your thoughts and concerns with God, ask questions, seek answers, and gain the wisdom of God. Through prayer, God will give you the wisdom, knowledge, direction and instructions that are necessary for walking wholly in your purpose. Prayer is critical for the success of purpose. You should start your day with prayer by thanking God for your purpose and for what He wants to accomplish through your life here on the earth. In prayer, you should ask for creative ideas, strategies, wisdom, and insight to carry out your purpose in your everyday life. It is best that you write down everything you ask and everything you hear from God.

When your purpose is revealed to you, it will be vitally important for you to keep it before you. This is the hard part because your purpose will only be developed by the work you put into it. You have what it takes to do what you were purposed to do, but you will have to give it everything you've got. *"…But he who gathers by labor will increase"* (Proverbs 13:1). It is vital that you work on yourself to the point where you become your purpose. Your purpose is not about you, but it is about what God wants to do through you. Even if you are further along in age, that doesn't mean that there is no longer a specific purpose for your life. For some of us, it may take longer to prepare for our purpose. Just know that preparation time is not lost time; God's timing is always perfect. You were created for a purpose, and God wants you to walk in it for the joy of others so that your joy may be fulfilled. *"For we are His workmanship, created in Christ Jesus for good works, which God prepared beforehand that we should walk in them"* (Ephesians 2:10).

Your gift, talent, skill, or ability is developed by the work you put into it. Growth in these areas helps with developing the full potential of your purpose. Maturation in life can be a result of the cultivation of purpose and the fulfilling of life's calling. Your skill or ability is designed to be given away, and you are establishing a life that has purposeful meaning when you do so. Purpose is designed to be useful and honorable with compassion to make a difference. *"The Lord will perfect that which concerns me; Your mercy endures forever; do not forsake the works of Your hands"* *(Psalms 138:8).* Many people can use their purpose to start a business, ministry, or impact in the marketplace and different industries. You must be sensitive to where God is leading you and where your purpose would be most effective. Trust God and where He is leading you because it is exactly where He wants you to be. *"The Lord is my rock and my fortress and my deliverer; My God, my strength, in whom I will trust..." (Psalms 18:2).*

This may be hard for us because this path is not going in the direction we want to go, or if it is where we want to go, it may not be at the pace we think it should be going. This journey in life and the journey to walking in purpose must be one of faith. It is a marathon and not a sprint. Our faith in God and His direction shows Him that we trust Him with our life. Walking by faith and trusting God's leading are intricate aspects of following the pathway that leads to purpose. *"For we walk by faith, not by sight. "(2 Corinthians 5:7).*

God gives us visions, dreams, and desires because they are impactful for His kingdom and His glory. Your desires should line up with His desires. As you spend time in the word of God, you will learn of the things that God desires, and your desires will be altered to match God's. God desires for people to forsake their ways and thoughts for His. This is done by allowing God's word to renew your mind and His spirit to dwell richly in you, which will allow Him to move through you. *"For My thoughts are not your thoughts, nor are your ways My ways, says the Lord," (Isaiah 55:7).* Allowing God's word to renew your mind and His spirit to have His way in your heart will cause the perfect alignment between your desires and God's desires. It is God's desire for people to be saved, to forsake their way, and to come into the knowledge and truth of His word. God does this through you when you yield your will to His will. *"For this is good and acceptable in the sight of God our Savior, who desires all men to be saved and to come to the knowledge of the truth...." (1 Timothy 2:3-4).*

You do not have to be a preacher to share the truth of God, just a willing vessel. If you have the skill of financial organization, you could meet someone who is in financial distress and has no clue what to do. Through your financial skillset, you can impart wisdom to that person to help them through their financial distress. God has utilized your skill to show compassion to someone and fulfill a purpose. You have to align your heart with the heart of God and have a burning passion for the things that God desires to be done in the earth. By being sensitive to the anointing of the spirit in your heart, you will want to fulfill God's desire and share His truth. Sharing the truth of God can be done simply by you walking in your purpose.

☙ Following Purpose ❧

*Listen to advice and accept discipline, and at the end you will be
counted among the wise. Many are the plans in a person's heart,
but it is the LORD's **purpose** that prevails.*
(Proverbs 19:20-21)

I blindly followed my ambition to be a background
dancer for a rapper and to be in music videos not readily
knowing the path that I would have to take to get there or
how far it would lead me away from my purpose. Many
people fall into the same traps. They are enticed and lured
away by their own passions and desires instead of openly
seeking God for what He desires for their life. God wants us
to be sensitive to our unique gifts and to use them to identify
our purpose. Don't blindly pursue an ambition because you
see something fun, heartfelt, or profitable in it, but pursue
the truth in discovering your God-given purpose and how
you can use it to glorify God.

Purpose is not tied to success; success comes from the
fulfillment of your God-ordained purpose, which leads to
the destiny God designed for you. Success manifests when
you align your thoughts, decisions, and actions to serve and
honor God. I know it may seem enticing to follow your
heart, do what you want to do, and to turn your *passion into
profit for* financial gain, but, in the end, that may not be
God's plan for your life. *"Many are the plans in a person's heart
but it is the Lord's purpose that prevails" (Proverbs 19:21).* I've

heard people who are walking in their purpose say that they love what they do not because it is what they get paid to do, but because it's what they're supposed to be doing, and they could do it for free.

When you tap into God's plan and purpose for your life, success, fulfillment, and financial prosperity are sure to follow. Don't get me wrong. God does not have a problem with you doing something that you desire or even turning your *passion into profits*, but that cannot become the central focus. *"Thus, says the Lord, your Redeemer, The Holy One of Israel: I am the Lord your God, who teaches you to profit..."* (Isaiah 48:17). *"And you shall remember the Lord your God, for it is He who gives you power to get wealth, that He may establish His covenant..."* (Deuteronomy 8:18). It is clear from these scriptures that God wants us to have financial success, but it is for His Kingdom, His glory, and His purpose.

When God is calling you to a certain place or level in your life, there is only one way and that is through your obedience. There cannot be any compromise when God is calling you to do something great. When you trust God, you will obey Him. Your principal focus should be the pursuit of God's purpose for your life because it is there that you will have the grace, strength, and ability to do what has been predestined for you. God wants you to take pleasure in the things of God and that which He desires for your life so that you may prosper in it. God is pleased when you prosper from your purpose because He is magnified in it. *"Let them shout for joy and be glad, who favor my righteous cause; And let them say continually, Let the Lord be magnified, who has pleasure in the prosperity of His servant"* (Psalms 35:27).

We were created to live outside of ourselves for the benefit of others. Our purpose in which we were created was fashioned in us before we were born, and it is developed as we go through life on the path directed by God. That purpose for which you were ordained is guaranteed to come to fruition if you will just walk in it. Your God-ordained, divinely-inspired purpose is the only thing in your life that will work exactly the way it is supposed to. Your unique purpose sets you apart from anyone and anything else.

Furthermore, your purpose must be protected at all cost. There is protection, provision, and prosperity within your unique purpose. You must release your faith to walk in it, and God's favor will bring it to pass. The job of the thief is to steal, kill, and destroy. Once purpose is identified and revealed, the enemy's agenda immediately goes into effect. He tries to steal our purpose by killing our self-worth, self-value, and self-esteem so that we feel like we have no purpose. He tries to destroy us by putting us in places and situations that move us further away from God and His purpose for our lives until it seems as if all is lost. But all is not lost. You are not replaceable. You are here for a reason. God created you for a purpose, and He wants you to have revelation of this. Revelation brings forth actions, and God wants you to act in accordance with His purpose and plan for you so that He can lead you to the destiny He intended for your life. God is waiting for you to find your purpose and to boldly live it out.

More important than any earthly purpose, there are distinctive spiritual purposes for our lives that we are expected to walk in as well. Simply going to church is not fulfilling purpose, even if you are serving in the church. There are many people who are in church serving relentlessly, and this may cause them to confuse their service in the local assembly as their purpose, which is not entirely accurate. God uses our gifts and talents within the local assembly for the purpose of fulfilling the vision assignment for that ministry. The purpose He preordained for each individual is meant to have a greater impact than serving within the four walls of the church; it is for the work of the ministry and building up the body of Christ. *"For the equipping of the saints for the work of ministry, for the edifying of the body of Christ" (Ephesians 4:12).* Working in ministry should not overshadow your purpose; they should work hand in hand. God wants to build the Kingdom of God and the body of Christ, and He does that through willing workers who yield to His purpose for their lives.

Thus, the number one spiritual purpose is to worship God. *"But the hour is coming, and now is, when the true worshipers will worship the Father in spirit and truth; for the Father is seeking such to worship Him. God is Spirit, and those who worship Him must worship in spirit and truth" (John 4:23-24).* Worship to God is essential because it keeps you in the presence of God where He can reveal instructions, give directions, and provide clarity for walking in your purpose.

Our next spiritual purpose is to be a disciple abiding in Christ, becoming like him, and making new disciples. *"Then Jesus said to those Jews who believed Him, if you abide in My word, you are My disciples indeed. And you shall know the truth, and the truth shall make you free" (John 8:31-32). "Go therefore and make disciples of all the nations, baptizing them in* the name of the Father and of the Son and of the Holy Spirit" (Matthew 28:19). As you are one who lives in Christ, it is expected for you to develop others to live in Christ also to fulfill the plan of God in the earth and to be fruitful and multiply. As you are fruitful in Christ, you are able to multiply through bringing others to Christ as well. *"By this My Father is glorified, that you bear much fruit; so you will be My disciples" (John 15:8).*

Another very important spiritual purpose is to serve God and do the work of the ministry, which includes serving others. *"How much more, then, will the blood of Christ, who through the eternal Spirit offered himself unblemished to God, cleanse our consciences from acts that lead to death so that we may serve the living God!" (Hebrews 9:14). "Each of you has been blessed with one of God's many wonderful gifts to be used in the service of others. So use your gift well" (1Peter 4:10).* Serving God must be a way of life. By walking in your purpose, it shows that you are serving God and doing the will of God. Serving God yields a benefit that the world cannot give. *"If they obey and serve Him, they shall spend their days in prosperity, And their years in pleasures" (Job 36:11).*

The spiritual purpose of Evangelism is also vital as it is completing Jesus' mission in the world. *"That is, that God was in Christ reconciling the world to Himself, not imputing their trespasses to them, and has committed to us the word of reconciliation. Now then, we are ambassadors for Christ, as though God were pleading through us: we implore you on Christ's behalf, be reconciled to God" (2 Corinthians 5:19-20).* It is not good that people live life outside of purpose, but it is worse if they are living life outside of God. Operating in the spiritual purpose of evangelism allows God to use you to share the gospel to reconcile the lost back to Him.

Your life is important to God, and you were created for His purpose. Therefore, you should be cognizant of your value so as to guard your life and preserve it for God's use and purpose. It is God's desire for His purpose for your life to be revealed and fulfilled. Hence, no matter what you may have done in the past or what you may presently be doing, God's love, forgiveness, grace, and mercy are available to lead you to be in right standing with Him and in the righteousness of God. I want you to be assured in knowing that God wants to use you. Your life is valuable and important to the work of the kingdom of God, and He wants to work through you. So, I implore you to yield yourself to the spirit of God and allow His purpose to be fulfilled in you. I encourage you to open your heart and let the light of the spirit of God illuminate your *"pathway to purpose"* so that others may see your good works and glorify God. *"Let your light so shine before men, that they may see your good works and glorify your Father in heaven" (Matthew 5:16).*

Afterword

I truly hope you were blessed and inspired by my story of discovering my *pathway to purpose*. This book has multiple purposes: to help you reflect on seeds that were sown into you in the past and determine if they have affected your path to purpose, assist you in being conscious of the seeds that were sown into you, help you be mindful of the situations or the circumstances that you allow in your lives, aid you with being aware of the tactics and decoys of the enemy, help you to learn from my mistakes to avoid the derailment from purpose, and lastly, help others seek God to determine their purpose.

It is my prayer and desire that this book will help you take a closer look at your life, examine the path you are on, and seek God in discovering your "original" purpose. Especially if you have taken a detour in your life's journey, if there have been decoys in your life, or if you've fallen victim to deception. You are more than capable of overcoming any challenge, situation, or circumstance that you may have faced in life if you make the decision to stand on the word of God. You must cast down every thought that is contrary to the word, develop patience, and stand firm in knowing who you are in Christ.

You don't necessarily have to have a great tribulation to have a great purpose. God can use the smallest trial, such as the loss of a job, or the greatest trial, such as the loss of a child, to lead to purpose. Don't think that purpose only comes through trials or tribulations. In some cases, those are used by God to show His goodness in people's lives and for the purpose of helping others overcome. *"These things I have spoken to you, that in Me you may have peace. In the world, you will have tribulation; but be of good cheer, I have overcome the world" (John 16:33).*

My story may be similar to someone else's story, but we each had different experiences and different outcomes. My story may touch, impact, or affect lives differently than another person who had a similar journey. There are numerous books out there on purpose and how to discover your purpose, but God gave me a specific and unique way that He wanted me to share my story. It is through my personal testimony of being blind to ambition that I may help someone who was in a similar situation. When God wants something done, all He is looking for is a willing vessel, and once He gets that, He has a way of making sure His will is done. *"For it is God who works in you both to will and to do for His good pleasure" (Philippians 2:13).*

I pray that you will discover your purpose and fulfill it to maximize God's glory and expand His kingdom with more people of purpose. I pray that you will be built up in faith to accomplish the purpose of God for your life. One way of accomplishing God's purpose is to know your purpose and to walk completely in it. You were created for God's purpose, and your chief goal in life should be to live to fulfill God's purpose and not your own agenda or that which the enemy has tried to set for you. *"Then God said, "Let Us make man in Our image, according to Our likeness; let them have dominion over the fish of the sea, over the birds of the air, and over the cattle, over all the earth and over every creeping thing that creeps on the earth." So, God created man in His own image; in the image of God He created him; male and female He created them. Then God blessed them, and God said to them, "Be fruitful and multiply; fill the earth and subdue it; have dominion over the fish of the sea, over the birds of the air, and over every living thing that moves on the earth" (Genesis 1:26-28).*

"Live life on purpose, for purpose; your destiny awaits you!"
Wendi Hayman

About the Author

Wendi Hayman is an author, publisher, dance minister, entrepreneur, wife, and mother. She is called to impact and advance the Kingdom as a prophetic voice of purpose. Her story is a long and winding road from the pole, to the pew, to God's purpose for her life. For many years, Wendi lived with guilt and embarrassment of past experiences as an adult entertainer and would not share her story with anyone. After finding freedom in Christ, she emerged out of hiding and moved forward beyond her past to empower women around the globe.

Work with Wendi
Wendi is a creative powerhouse, who uses her passions to help others and advance the kingdom of God. As a speaker, writer, and dancer, Wendi works closely with ministry leaders, aspiring authors and mission-driven entrepreneurs in a variety of ways.

Speaking
Women of all ages relate to Wendi's transparent truth, *Blind Ambition*, of seeking validity in the wrong places until finally discovering her purpose. Wendi speaks on the following topics to women and young adult audiences in business, entrepreneurship, schools, community and women's organizations.
- Recovering from Life's Pitfalls
- Giving God the Best You (Purpose & Vision Talk)

* Sharing your Testimony, Confidently & Boldly

Ghostwriting and Publishing

As the Creative Director of *Glory to Glory* Publications, LLC, Wendi enjoys helping aspiring authors write and publish their books. She has created a stress-free ghostwriting process to take authors from book idea to implementation.

Dancing

Wendi is a Dance Minister and the founder of W.A.R. Prophetic Dance Ministry, a liturgical dance company. In this capacity, she trains ministry dancers and travels throughout the nation, performing at churches and private events.

Send booking inquiries to: wendihayman@gmail.com.

For more information visit online at:
www.wendihayman.com
wendihayman@gmail.com
info@glorytoglorypublications.com
Facebook: Wendi Hayman
Instagram: @wendihayman
Periscope: Wendi Hayman
Twitter: Hayman_Wendi

Other Books by Wendi Hayman

bit.ly/OneHotSummer

Made in the USA
Middletown, DE
18 June 2022

67355442R00086